I0796262

POCKET PORTRAITS

JANE AUSTEN

The Original Romance Novelist

JANET LEWIS SAIDI

ADAMS MEDIA
NEW YORK AMSTERDAM/ANTWERP LONDON TORONTO
SYDNEY/MELBOURNE NEW DELHI

For Christy, "such a Sister."

Adams Media
An Imprint of Simon & Schuster, LLC
100 Technology Center Drive
Stoughton, MA 02072

First Adams Media hardcover edition September 2025

Interior design by Kellie Emery
Illustrations by Kim Arrington
Interior images © Adobe Stock/Helga

Manufactured in the United States of America

10 9 8 7 6 5 4 3 2 1

Library of Congress Control Number: 2025940125

ISBN 978-1-5072-2415-1
ISBN 978-1-5072-2416-8 (ebook)

Acknowledgments

There are so many people to be grateful for:

All the Janeites for the Austen discussions you convene: podcasters Emily Davis-Hale, Lauren Wethers, Diane Neu, and Zan Cammack. And Sarah Rose Kearns, Tabrizia Jones, Maria DeBlassie, Susan Allen Ford, Nikki Payne, Cathy Stubbs, Devoney Looser, and the late Patrick McGraw, who brought so many of us joy through Jane Austen.

For early readers and supporters of this book: Diane Neu, Emily Davis-Hale, Andrea Heiss, and Nancy West.

For the KBIA News team: Katelynn, Stan, Anna, Becky, Jana Rose, and Harshawn—who heard many Austen updates at news meetings.

For brilliant friends and colleagues: Jackie Bell, Debra Mason, Ronna Birenbaum, Eilene Zimmerman, Kara Edgerson, Reuben Stern, Ruth Gallant, Allie Gassmann, Claire Marie Mallory, Lee Wilkins, Steve Weinberg, Brenda Spell, Sherri Oliver, Jana Dierker, Jim Ely, Michael Gallagher, Paetra Serra, April Watson, Sara Hiles, Kathy Kiely, Nina Mukerjee Furstenau, Stephanie Shonekan, and Tina Casagrand Foss.

Thanks to my agent, Andy Ross, and the awesome Adams Media editors Colleen Mulhern and Sarah Doughty.

For my family of The Lewis Farm Thing—you know who you are—especially Larry and Mary for all the book conversations at the lake.

For Mark, an amazing scholar, writer, and brother.

For Dad and bonus-mom Creda, whose capacity for happy marriage might shock Austen.

For Dara and the Saidi sisters Samira, Suzanne, and Nada. Sisters are the best.

For my sister, Christy, who is both the most soulful and the funniest person I know. And for Anna, who calls me just to talk about Jane Austen novels.

For Riad—always as challenging, as intriguing, and as loving as any Austen hero.

And for Catherine and Miriam: You are the lights of my life.

Table of Contents

Introduction

After more than two centuries, six novels, and countless adaptations of her life story and works, many fans believe they know Jane Austen. Born in 1775 in a Hampshire parsonage, Austen would go on to write classics, like *Pride and Prejudice* and *Emma,* that have made her one of the most important English novelists of all time. She created romantic plots that feature marriage, money, and society, and perfected that fictional resolution known today as the happily-ever-after. But you may be surprised to learn there is more to Jane Austen's story than bonnets and handsome suitors. . . .

In *Pocket Portraits: Jane Austen,* you'll dig deeper into her life and works. Here, you'll explore one hundred biographical vignettes that peer into the world of Jane Austen, from her early years in eighteenth-century England, to her lasting impact on pop culture. Uncover details about:

- An engagement that lasted for just one day, and other disappointments in her own love life
- The publication of her first major success, *Sense and Sensibility*, under the mysterious byline "By a Lady"
- The challenges of displacement that followed her father's death
- The countless letters that her sister burned after her passing . . . and theories surrounding why
- And much more

You'll also find excerpts of her works, including her juvenilia as well as novels like *Persuasion* and *Mansfield Park*, and quotes from her correspondence with friends and family.

From Austen's thoughts on high society, to how her bond with her own sister shaped the sisterhood of *Sense and Sensibility*'s Elinor and Marianne Dashwood, you'll explore defining themes in her life through her works and surviving letters. Turn the page to unravel the life, the love, and the audacity of a young Regency woman who became one of the most celebrated authors of fiction and romance.

A Single Mother Makes Her Way

For generations, members of Jane Austen's family were hard workers. They had no choice: Her father, George Austen, had to look after himself from boyhood, as had his father and, before him, his grandmother, Elizabeth Austen.

Jane Austen's great-grandmother, Elizabeth Austen (born Elizabeth Weller), was a gentleman's daughter who married John Austen, the son of a wealthy cloth manufacturer, in 1693. They then moved to a manor house, Broadford, in Horsmonden and had seven children. When John died of tuberculosis in 1704, around the age of thirty-four (just one year before his own father), Elizabeth was left with a house full of children, some pre-marriage debts accumulated by her husband, and a deathbed promise from her relatives that she and her children would be looked after.

But that promise failed. Left on her own with the younger six children to provide for—the eldest would inherit the estate—Elizabeth took a step down the social ladder and hired herself as a housekeeper to the master of a schoolhouse. After selling her household silver and linens and taking up a post at the schoolhouse in Sevenoaks, Kent, she managed to settle her husband's debts by 1708. She also arranged for her six children to get a solid education as part of her housekeeping position.

At a time when systems of inheritance, primogeniture, and coverture placed the lives of women largely in the hands of husbands or male relatives, Elizabeth successfully pursued one thing for her children that could get a young person by in the eighteenth century: education.

Elizabeth's hardships were passed along to her son William and his son George, Jane Austen's father (explored later in this book). But other things were also passed along, including Elizabeth's belief in education and her strength of character. If Elizabeth Austen could have looked into a crystal ball and seen one hundred years into the future, she'd find her great-granddaughter, Jane Austen, similarly making use of hard work and education to improve her circumstances. And Jane's work would include heroines who made use of those same resources: education, integrity—and imagination. But more on that later!

THE MORE YOU KNOW

Most of what is known of Elizabeth Austen's ordeal comes from a compilation of family letters known as the *Austen Papers*. In order to generate income, Elizabeth wrote in a letter to her father, she had to sell her households goods, such as the "furniture of my best chamber, my [silver] plate and all the rest of my household linen."

George and Cassandra

In 1775, a rectory near the village of Steventon in rural Hampshire was home to a lively household. The Reverend George Austen—grandson to Elizabeth—and his wife, Cassandra, were raising four sons and a daughter (also named Cassandra), with another daughter (to be named Jane) on the way. A fifth son, George, was being raised away from home, due to developmental disabilities including epilepsy and deafness. As biographer Claire Tomalin paints the picture, also being raised on the parsonage grounds and its surrounding farmland were crops of wheat, hops, and barley—all tended by George and Cassandra. Additionally, the Steventon rectory did the business of water hauling, linen washing, and keeping a vegetable garden, dairy cows, and a poultry yard.

But going back to the 1750s, you would find a young Cassandra visiting St. John's College, Oxford, where her uncle was the prestigious Master of Balliol. One of the more impressive divinity students there was George Austen, known on campus as "the handsome proctor." Largely left to fend for himself after the death of his father, George would find in an Oxford education a kind of landing place, providing the mentorship and support between the fellows of St. John's College missing in his life so far. At the top of his class, he was ordained in 1755 during his time at the college, and served as the assistant chaplain and Junior Proctor, eventually receiving a Bachelor of Arts, and then a Master of Arts.

There's no record of just how George and Cassandra crossed paths, though some believe her uncle may have introduced the two. However they met, marriage and family were somewhat of a luxury for younger sons of the eighteenth-century English gentry who didn't inherit. So even though George had been ordained in 1755, George and Cassandra didn't marry until he had obtained a "living" and taken up the post of rector of Steventon. On April 26, 1764, the handsome proctor and his bride were married at St. Swithin's, in Bath. Mirroring their life to come, it was a practical affair: In attendance were a few family members. The service was officiated by a friend of the bride, who wore a red dress of sturdy wool, suitable for traveling, cut in the style of a riding habit.

The More You Know

The Jane Austen's House museum describes George Austen during his time at Oxford as: "Tall, slim, and good-looking with chestnut brown hair and bright, hazel eyes." Cassandra Leigh was "clever and witty," enjoyed writing poetry, and was born the fifth child of six. Clergy "livings" were incomes that were held by landowners and members of the gentry and aristocracy as patrons—many of the English Great Houses maintained one or two of them, as did Oxford and Cambridge Universities.

A House Full of Boys

Jane Austen was born into an unusual household: Steventon rectory not only housed four brothers—James, Edward, Henry, and Frank—with their sister, Cassandra, but also doubled as a school for boys. Like George's grandmother before him, the Austens would take in students and conduct lessons out of their home. They valued a strong education, and the Steventon parsonage was filled with books and a love for reading. Rev. Austen's library held some five hundred volumes; the family spent many evenings reading together aloud from his collection. Austen refers in her letters to her father reading aloud in the evening and describes her family as "great novel-readers and not ashamed of being so." All this made the Austen family a little ahead of their time in a key way: They valued imagination, novels, and education in service of a meritocracy.

Jane's brothers James and Henry would both follow in their father's footsteps to become fellows at St. John's College, Oxford, while her youngest brothers, Frank and Charles, each entered the Naval College at Portsmouth at the age of twelve and rose through the ranks during his lifetime. As mentioned earlier in this book, the second-oldest brother, George, was developmentally disabled and was raised by family friends away from home. (George was deaf, which may be why Jane Austen appeared to know the deaf alphabet.) The third eldest brother, Edward, was adopted at the age of sixteen by distant cousins to be the heir to their estates, including Chawton and Godmersham.

Rev. and Mrs. Austen were creative and alert to how to leverage their resources and connections to benefit their family and provide for them. At a time when a meritocracy wasn't really viewed as an ideal way of life for the gentry (or girls), Jane Austen's girlhood played out against a backdrop of boys, books, and debate. Her upbringing included a rigorous education—not only in conventional subjects like history, literature, and language, but also in teasing and joking, an aspect of life at Steventon that would make a striking appearance in her early notebooks, and in a lifetime of letters and fiction writing to come!

THE MORE YOU KNOW

The Reverend George Austen wrote in a letter about Jane's birth on December 16, 1775: "She is to be Jenny . . . " "Jenny" was christened by her father immediately, at home, just like her older brothers and sister had been. Biographer Claire Tomalin notes that Cassandra and her baby would have spent the early weeks of their life together in a four-poster bed of the first-floor bedroom, where Cassandra likely nursed her new baby for a good three months before possibly sending her out, as her siblings had been, for nurturing by a village family.

Formal Education

Education is one of the most important themes in all of Jane Austen's works, and it was also one of the most important topics of the eighteenth-century world she was growing up in. Jane Austen's own experience with education was decidedly mixed: At the age of seven (1783), she and Cassandra were sent to Mrs. Cawley's school in Oxford, where their brothers studied. But later that same year, Mrs. Cawley moved to Southampton, taking Jane, Cassandra, and their cousin Jane Cooper (Mrs. Cawley's niece), with her. As writer Deirdre Le Faye wrote in her *A Family Record,* Southampton was full of British troops returning from sea—and bringing typhus fever with them. Both Cassandra and Jane became infected, and when Mrs. Cawley didn't raise the alarm with their parents, Jane Cooper took it upon herself to write home. All three girls were rescued by Mrs. Austen and Jane's mother, Mrs. Cooper. Tragically, once all were safe home, Mrs. Cooper, who had become infected herself, died.

Two years later, in the spring of 1785, the idea of education was renewed and the Austens planned to send Cassandra to school. According to family lore, Jane insisted on going as well and the two sisters attended Abbey House School in Reading, situated between Hampshire and Oxford, at the site of a ruined abbey. According to Le Faye, they learned literary arts, dancing arts, French, and needlework, all from Mrs. La Tournelle, whose real name was Sarah Hackitt and who didn't speak a word of French. The girls also had plenty of time to chat with their friends and socialize among the house and gardens during their time at the boarding school. They returned home after one year at Abbey House School.

LITERARY CONNECTIONS

Even though Jane Austen and her sister Cassandra had only a few years of formal education at the two boarding schools, Jane read widely, observed the characters of those around her, and worked to apply her wide readings to her life and art. In this pursuit, she had the benefit of a major influencer, writer, and thinker who was born sixteen years before her: Mary Wollstonecraft. A political philosopher, Mary Wollstonecraft called for equality in education practices in her 1792 *A Vindication of the Rights of Woman*. She demanded for women to not just be passive, elegant, pretty things, but to be educated and trained equally. Otherwise, she reasoned, what a waste of half the population and its resources!

The Beautiful Cassandra

By the time Jane turned twelve years old (December 1787) she had begun to create stories and spoofs in a notebook labeled *Volume the First.* Among this first collection is a tribute titled "The beautifull [sic] Cassandra." This was no ordinary tale: The young Jane was already lampooning the self-righteousness and grandiosity of the era's sentimental novels. Her "beautifull" Cassandra steals pastries, knocks people over, and falls in love with a bonnet. In this short, condensed parody of a novel, the heroine ostensibly leads the life of a Regency young lady while overturning conventions—both of society and of novels.

Jane's relationship with her sister, Cassandra Elizabeth Austen, inspired the tale of "The beautifull Cassandra." The two siblings were close; in fact, most of the 161 surviving letters of Jane Austen are addressed to her older sister, discussing the visits, walks, balls, parties, and people the Austens encountered, and also Jane's daily concerns, sarcasms, and judgments. The relationship and her writing of "The beautifull Cassandra" would eventually lead Austen to her first published novel: *Sense and Sensibility.* Explored further later in this book, *Sense and Sensibility* follows two sisters with different dispositions, each seeking love amid family and societal pressures, united by their shared values and affection.

By 1795, seven years after Jane wrote her tale, the "beautifull" real-life Cassandra traded in her passion for bonnets and embarked on an engagement to a young man named Tom, a former pupil at the rectory. Tom became the Reverend Tom Fowle, and set sail for the West Indies. But sadly, the engagement lasted barely two years: In 1797, Tom died near Santo Domingo and was buried at sea. Cassandra would never marry.

LITERARY CONNECTIONS

Nearly all the juvenilia in Jane Austen's notebooks are dedicated to her circle of family members, neighbors, and friends. In the parodic "The History of England," Cassandra steps out as an artist to produce thirteen miniature portraits of England's monarchs that resemble members of the Austen family more than the monarchs themselves in a mash-up of history, biography, and wit. The work is attributed to "a partial, prejudiced, & ignorant Historian," with this parenthetical note: "There will be very few Dates in this History."

From "The beautifull Cassandra"

When Cassandra had attained her 16th year, she was lovely and amiable and chancing to fall in love with an elegant Bonnet, her Mother had just completed bespoke by the Countess of —she placed it on her gentle Head and walked from her Mother's shop to make her Fortune.

Introducing the Austen Family Barn Theater

At the same time that young Jane was writing her first stories about characters like the "beautifull" Cassandra, a fascinating character entered her real world. The setting was Steventon Rectory, Christmastime, 1787. The students at the rectory had left to spend the holidays with their families, and in their place the Austen family was hosting George's sister Philadelphia and her daughter, Eliza (aka the Comtesse de Feuillide).

Eliza's life to this point was like a Regency-era adventure narrative. When George and Philadelphia were left orphaned and mostly unprovided for by family, Philadelphia had few options as a woman in England. After being apprenticed to a milliner at the age of fifteen, she decided to travel to India. There she married a British employee of the East India Company, Tysoe Saul Hancock, and gave birth to Eliza. Born in Calcutta, India, and raised in London, France, and Germany, Eliza was accomplished in playing musical instruments, enjoyed dancing and the theater, and spoke multiple languages. She was also married to a count, and arrived at Steventon in 1787 with her French baby and heir, Hastings

Francois Louis Eugène Capot de Feuillide. Jane and her siblings were enchanted by their older cousin and her adventurous life.

Together, Jane, her siblings, and Eliza transformed the Steventon barn into a theater and started to rehearse playwright Susanna Centlivre's *The Wonder: A Woman Keeps a Secret*. This 1714 romantic comedy features a gregarious leading lady, Violante, secretly hiding her best friend, also the sister of her lover, Felix, to protect her from an overbearing father and his marriage plans for her. The result is Shakespearean shenanigans, hide-and-seek antics, jealousies, and confusions. The Austen family production cast Eliza as the flirtatious Violante. Opposite her was Henry—by all accounts charming, playful, and tall. These theatrics are believed to have made a big impression on Jane, who was already taking to her notebook, *Volume the First*, to pen her own stories of heroines, heroes, and courtship mishaps.

LITERARY CONNECTIONS

Jane Austen's early stories are dedicated to a few of the key players in the Austen family's production of *The Wonder: A Woman Keeps a Secret*: her brother Henry; sister, Cassandra; and cousin Eliza. The loving, mocking dedications are now viewed by fans and scholars as valuable little gifts to time, showing in Jane a talent for humor, a fondness for in-jokes and shockers, and a lot of writing promise.

"Henry and Eliza" and Henry and Eliza

The theatricals of the Austen family Christmases provided material for Jane's notebook *Volume the First*. One tale particularly stands out: "Henry and Eliza." This story features a beautiful heroine, Eliza, who deploys her considerable charms to successfully garner the support of a Lady Harriet, then cons her and runs away with this grand lady's lover, Mr. Cecil. A short note is left for Lady Harriet: "MADAM/ We are married and gone./HENRY AND ELIZA CECIL."

In the coming months, the real Eliza would return to Paris, where France was experiencing a hard winter, with famine and starvation in the countryside. In July 1789, the storming of the Bastille would launch the French Revolution. Then, in 1793, war broke out between France and England, and by 1794, Eliza's husband, Jean-François Capot de Feuillide, had been arrested and guillotined. After twelve years of marriage, and at the age of thirty-three, this lively cousin who had brought the outside world to the Steventon parsonage was a widow.

One year later, Henry, who had left Oxford just before his ordination to join the Oxfordshire Militia, was a lieutenant in a red coat. He sought out Eliza and proposed, only to be turned down. Two years after this, Eliza was courted by James Austen, only to eventually refuse him as well! However, in 1797, Henry and Eliza would find their way back to each other and marry, at St. Marylebone Parish Church in London. At the time of their marriage, Henry was twenty-six and Eliza thirty-six with access to an inheritance.

LITERARY CONNECTIONS

Jane Austen's cousin Eliza is thought to have been the inspiration for the lively, mercenary heroine of *Lady Susan,* Austen's hilariously amoral, anarchic novella. Lady Susan Vernon is the ultimate anti-heroine: promiscuous, ruthless, and ambitious—even to the point of exploiting her daughter, the real heroine of this story.

From "Henry and Eliza"

Eliza, being perfectly conscious of the derangement in their affairs, immediately on her Husband's death set sail for England, in a man of War of 55 Guns, which they had built in their more prosperous Days. But no sooner had she stepped on Shore at Dover, with a Child in each hand, than she was seized by the officers of the Dutchess, and conducted by them to a snug little Newgate of their Lady's which she had erected for the reception of her own private Prisoners.

Volumes the Second and Third

Up through 1793, Jane Austen continued to write stories and comical sketches in a set of notebooks. Following *Volume the First* came *Volume the Second* and *Volume the Third,* which offered more parodic dedications to family members, sarcastic commentaries on the world around her, and chaotic plots. The stories were usually signed "Your most grateful humble Servant The Author"—or something similar.

Known by scholars today as the juvenilia, the contents of Austen's notebooks are praised for their virtuosity and subversiveness. At first, they appear to imitate the flowery, melodramatic language of popular eighteenth-century writers like Samuel Richardson, Oliver Goldsmith, or Johann Wolfgang von Goethe, but time and again each story takes a swerve into absurdity, throwing aside conventional expectations in favor of the arbitrary, violence, adultery, and anarchy. The same themes of Richardson's popular *Pamela* are there: virtue, friendship, a public-private self and correspondence, the education of women, morals, and love. . . . But Austen twists them with satiric humor similar to author Henry Fielding's style in his parodic *The History of Tom Jones, A Foundling.*

One example is the parody from *Volume the Second* titled "A Letter from a Young Lady." The letter begins "Many have been the cares and vicissitudes of my past life," and then veers into absurdity: "I murdered my father at a very early period of my Life, I have since murdered my Mother, and I am now going to murder my Sister." The narrator of this story weaves a wild tale of perjury, stolen inheritance, and fake courtship, then circles back with the ending lines: "I am now going to murder my Sister. Yours Ever, Anna Parker."

LITERARY CONNECTIONS

One of Jane Austen's works of juvenilia, *Lady Susan*, would be adapted into a 2016 film titled *Love & Friendship*. The director, Whit Stillman, says "that was probably a mistake," since "Love & Freindship [sic]" was a different juvenile story by Austen. Regardless, it was a successful adaptation, starring Kate Beckinsale as the seductive Lady Susan Vernon. Beckinsale would also play Emma Woodhouse in a 1996 adaptation of Austen's *Emma*.

A Family of Writers

Jane's family was involved with her literary pursuits and young Austen was encouraged in her art! In fact, *Volume the Second* contains an inscription Jane had written as a heading on the contents page: "*Ex dono mei Patris*," which is Latin for "a gift from my father." Given the volume's content of family mix-ups, misunderstandings, and betrayals, some might assume this was sarcasm. But later, when Jane would pen her manuscript *First Impressions* (ultimately published as *Pride and Prejudice*), her father would send the manuscript to a publisher with a note requesting serious consideration of the anonymous work for publication. It would be "Declined by Return of Post," but shows her family's enthusiasm for her creations.

And vice versa: During the same time that Jane was writing her juvenilia, she is thought to also have been reading and reacting to her brothers' articles in their satirical periodical, *The Loiterer*. Written between 1789 and 1790 while James and Henry were attending Oxford, these articles by the Austen brothers satirize both university life and the conventions of the novels of the era. *The Loiterer* promised a "Rough, but not entirely inaccurate Sketch of the Character, the Manners, and the Amusement of Oxford . . . " Content was provided by the Austen brothers with their friends and a cousin, Edward Cooper. Sixty issues were published in total, until James left university.

Sending up, satirizing, and reading novels appears to have been a beloved pastime of the Austen household. Eventually, Jane's notebooks added up to about 74,000 words, created in a home that drew on playfulness and irreverence to challenge the ways people live and how life is depicted through story.

LITERARY CONNECTIONS

A pseudonymous letter in James and Henry Austen's *The Loiterer* reads a lot like their younger sister's sarcastic writing style. In this letter from "Sophia Sentiment," the author complains that while visiting Oxford, she was "dragged through dirty chapels, dusty libraries, and greasy halls." Though the true identity of Sophia Sentiment is still not confirmed, editor Christine Alexander found it likely enough to be a young Jane Austen that it's included in an appendix to her collection of Austen's juvenilia, *Love and Freindship* [sic] *and Other Youthful Writings.*

Lady Susan

Jane Austen's novella, *Lady Susan,* is estimated to have been written in 1794, when she was nineteen years old, and beginning to move from her notebooks of teen writings into story writing. The structure for *Lady Susan* follows a letter-writing (epistolary) format, detailing the story of one very awful mother, Lady Susan Vernon. A recent widow, Lady Susan is a known flirt in England, blatantly pursuing lovers like the married Mr. Manwaring. And now she's going after the young, dashing, well-born, and well-intentioned Reginald De Courcy, while simultaneously trying to marry off her intelligent daughter Frederica to an older, rich aristocrat. Meanwhile, Frederica has feelings for Reginald De Courcy herself!

The story, which unfolds through the correspondence of Lady Susan with various friends and family members, has all of Austen's favorite themes from her later novels—taking them to the utmost extreme. Austen uses irony, parody, and humor (which will become her trademarks) to force readers to look deeper into marriage customs, outward status symbols, class hierarchies, and outrageously bad behavior.

It all works out fine in the end for Lady Susan (and her daughter). Lady Susan marries Sir James, her daughter's unwanted suitor, while Frederica stays at Churchill with her true love interest, Reginald De Courcy. In the conclusion of this story, readers can see a transition from the more random structures of her juvenilia to the tightly constructed narratives of her later novels. The conclusion of *Lady Susan* showcases characteristics that will become key to all of Austen's endings—including an outcome that avoids extremes; a move toward elegant syntax ("She had nothing against her, but her Husband, and her Conscience"); a reference to information and belief ("The World must judge from Probability . . . "); and an aside from the narrator, directly addressing the reader ("Whether Lady Susan was, or was not happy in her second Choice—I do not see how it can ever be ascertained—").

The More You Know

The novella *Lady Susan* was written out in a "fair copy," or a final, corrected copy possibly with an intention to publish the story around 1805. But the story wouldn't be published until 1871, in the second edition of Austen nephew James Edward Austen-Leigh's *A Memoir of Jane Austen*. It included unpublished writings such as the original ending of *Persuasion*, the abandoned novel *The Watsons*, and the novel fragment known as *Sanditon*. While gathering materials for his memoir, James Edward corresponded with his sister, Austen niece Caroline Lefroy, who wrote that she preferred that the later teenaged writings like *Lady Susan* not to be published, calling them "betweenities."

From Lady Susan, Letter 31

Lady Susan to Mrs. Johnson
Upper Seymour St.

My dear Friend,

That tormenting creature Reginald is here. My Letter, which was intended to keep him longer in the Country, has hastened him to Town. Much as I wish him away however, I cannot help being pleased with such a proof of attachment. He is devoted to me, heart and soul—He will carry this note himself, which is to serve as an Introduction to you, with whom he longs to be acquainted. Allow him to spend the Evening with you, that I may be in no danger of his returning here.—I have told him that I am not well, and must be alone—and should he call again there might be confusion, for it is impossible to be sure of servants.—Keep him therefore I entreat you in Edward st.—You will not find him a heavy companion, and I allow you to flirt with him as much as you like.

Breaking the Fourth Wall

When teenaged Jane Austen put down her notebook of juvenilia and embarked on more in-depth stories, she used an epistolary structure of letter-writing to present the pursuits of Lady Susan. It's one of many aspects of storytelling in novels that Austen will boldly innovate throughout her career, taking it to new heights and creating the standard that would shape writers coming after her, from Henry James and James Joyce to Virginia Woolf and Marcel Proust.

In fact, Austen would become so accomplished at creating a believable, imaginary universe, that she would even take the opportunity to undermine the world she created! In each and every one of her novels' happy endings, Austen slows down the pacing, interrupts the narrative, and speaks directly to the reader with comments such as one in *Northanger Abbey* that tells readers they "will see by the tell-tale compression of the pages" that the characters are "hastening together to perfect felicity."

Breaking that fourth wall—the imaginary barrier between the narrator and the audience—is something Austen would have experienced during this time through reading Shakespeare, most famously Hamlet's famous interrogation of his audience with the question, "To be, or not to be, that is the question . . . " Building on early examples like this one, she created her own interruptions to pause her stories and draw attention to the process of story itself, readers' expectations of it, and systems of perception and belief—all starting with her early drafts! Through techniques like meta-fictional asides, her first steps into novel writing were adding up to an author ahead of her time. Her wit in breaking the fourth wall would echo in other works in the centuries to come, from Charlotte Brontë's line, "Reader, I married him" in *Jane Eyre* (1847), to Dakota Johnson's direct addresses to the audience as Anne Elliot in *Persuasion* (2022).

LITERARY CONNECTIONS

The term "Janeite"—signaling devotees of Jane Austen—dates back to an 1894 introduction to *Pride and Prejudice* by the British critic George Saintsbury. But it's better known from a story called "The Janeites" published in 1924 by Rudyard Kipling. The story is a relic from Britain's colonial past, featuring two ex-soldiers, one of whom served in Palestine, and showing how the soldiers have gained a sort of solidarity akin to freemasonry, through common reading of the works of Jane Austen.

"Profligate and Shocking" Lessons in Flirting

Similar to her fictional stories, young Jane Austen's very first preserved letter contains a blend of humor, observation, and gossip. Sitting in the Steventon parsonage in January 1796, twenty-year-old Jane wrote to her sister, Cassandra, who had just turned twenty-three, saying, "In the first place I hope you will live twenty-three years longer." By this time, Cassandra was engaged to the Reverend Tom Fowle. And while she and Jane would continue living together throughout the engagement (and the rest of Jane's life), they were often apart, visiting with family and friends. The sisters stayed in regular contact during these times, writing letters back and forth. Cassandra was now off for a visit while Jane kept her updated on life at Steventon.

The big news of Jane's letter was a ball held in honor of a Mr. Tom Lefroy the night before. She wrote that, this "very gentlemanlike, good-looking, pleasant young man" was a young Irish visitor to the neighborhood. Jane was "almost afraid" to give an account of her behavior at the ball but called on her sister to tap into her imagination: "Imagine to yourself everything most profligate and shocking," she wrote, "in the way of dancing and sitting down together."

Jane and a young gentleman dancing and sitting down together at a chaperoned neighborhood ball was not particularly "profligate," and much of this narrative reflects Austen's trademark sarcasm. But it's also possible that the pair *were* pushing the boundaries of acceptable Regency conduct. Describing another couple flirting at the ball, Jane wrote that they could take lessons from herself on how "to be particular." Jane also joked that Tom was wearing a white coat like that worn by author Henry Fielding's eponymous hero Tom Jones: "He is a very great admirer of Tom Jones," she wrote, "and therefore wears the same coloured clothes, I imagine, which *he* did when he was wounded" (a reference to Fielding's hero's blood-soaked white coat).

But Jane's adventure with Lefroy was short-lived. In a letter to Cassandra begun five days later, she wrote that Tom was leaving the neighborhood: "At length the Day is come on which I am to flirt my last with Tom Lefroy. . . . My tears flow as I write, at the melancholy idea."

THE MORE YOU KNOW

The Lefroy and Austen family narratives were deeply intertwined. In 1814, Jane's niece, Anna, married Tom Lefroy's cousin, Ben.

Playing Wallflower at the Kempshott Ball

Throughout her early twenties, Jane Austen's letters from Steventon Rectory continued with lively descriptions of the close-knit Hampshire social scene. One day, in January 1799, Jane wrote to her sister, Cassandra, who was staying at their brother Edward's estate of Godmersham, that she was attending a ball—"the Ball at Kempshott"—that evening. (At this point, her sister's fiancé had passed away.) Their younger brother, Charles, would be visiting Jane, and she had gotten an invitation to the ball for him as well, but had "not been so considerate as to get him a Partner." Jane noted that there was a "want of chairs" to accommodate everyone and more "Dancers than the Room could conveniently hold, which is enough to constitute a good Ball at any time."

The image of the crowded room she described to Cassandra is much like her description of the crowded balls of *Northanger Abbey*, which she was writing around this time (more on this later). In *Northanger Abbey*, a young Catherine Morland is jostled among strangers, only to be left standing in "discredit," as she believes, with those who have not been invited to dance. These feelings of being passed over, of being marginalized in a crowded room and a status-conscious space, will come up again and again in Austen's writings—both in her novels and in her letters.

Jane continued her January 1799 letter by admitting: "I do not think I was very much in request.—People were rather apt not to ask me till they could not help it;—One's Consequence you know varies so much at times without any particular reason—. There was one Gentleman, an officer of the Cheshire, a very good looking young Man, who I was told wanted very much to be introduced to me;—but as he did not want it quite enough to take much trouble in effecting it, We never could bring it about." Here Austen shared her disappointment in the constraints of a Regency world where young women didn't have the power to choose and where so much is left to timing, and fate.

LITERARY CONNECTIONS

In Jane Austen's novels, the women do have the power of refusal, but sometimes their refusals are ignored by men who won't take no for an answer. This includes *Northanger Abbey*'s John Thorpe, who refuses to let the main character, Catherine Morland, out of his carriage. When Catherine "intreated" him to stop, he laughed and "smacked his whip."

Northanger Abbey

Austen began writing her novel *Northanger Abbey*, finishing it around 1798 or 1799, when she was just twenty-three or twenty-four. (She had also started two other manuscripts that she would revise over the next decade: *Elinor and Marianne*, which would become *Sense and Sensibility*, and *First Impressions*, which would become *Pride and Prejudice*—but more on those later!)

Northanger Abbey not only takes readers on an adventure of gothic fantasy across England, but also examines the very concept and status of novels and novelists in the Regency era. The novel was still a new, and innovative, artistic endeavor at the time, and Austen's exploration of how novels work started in the first chapter—in fact, in the first sentence—of *Northanger Abbey*. The first sentence introduces the heroine, Catherine Morland: "No one who had ever seen Catherine Morland in her infancy would have supposed her born to be an heroine."

The chapter proceeds with a list of reasons why this heroine is not very heroic. Namely, unlike the gothic novel's usual pale, accomplished heroines battling evil circumstances and tragic beginnings, Catherine Morland has "dark, lank hair," sensible parents, a mild disposition, and a stable country home. She also prefers boys' games like "base ball" and "rolling down the green slope at the back of the house" to the more "ladylike" interests of heroines in this time period, mirroring Jane's own childhood at Steventon. Austen defies expectations in the creation of one of her very first heroines. She even throws in what is thought to be an in-joke: the name of Catherine Morland's father is Richard, an inexplicable Austen family joke from Jane's letters.

Toward the end of *Northanger Abbey*'s first chapter, there's a shift in Catherine's luck: She may not be a heroine, but as she approaches the age of seventeen she becomes a heroine-in-training. "Something must and will happen," the narrator assures readers in *Northanger Abbey*, "to throw a hero in her way."

The More You Know

First titled *Susan, Northanger Abbey* wouldn't be published until 1817, after Jane Austen's death. The publication was arranged by her brother, Henry, who changed the novel's title to *Northanger Abbey* and included a preface identifying Austen as the author of her novels. This would be the first time her identity was made public.

From Northanger Abbey, Chapter 1

What a strange, unaccountable character!—for with all these symptoms of profligacy at ten years old, she had neither a bad heart nor a bad temper, was seldom stubborn, scarcely ever quarrelsome, and very kind to the little ones, with few interruptions of tyranny; she was moreover noisy and wild, hated confinement and cleanliness, and loved nothing so well in the world as rolling down the green slope at the back of the house. Such was Catherine Morland at ten. At fifteen, appearances were mending; she began to curl her hair and long for balls; her complexion improved, her features were softened by plumpness and colour, her eyes gained more animation, and her figure more consequence. Her love of dirt gave way to an inclination for finery, and she grew clean as she grew smart; she had now the pleasure of sometimes hearing her father and mother remark on her personal improvement.

Father Austen versus Father Tilney

All the evidence suggests that Jane Austen had a good father. He was an early supporter of her love for writing, gifting her with the notebook that became *Volume the Second*. And when *First Impressions* was mostly finished, it was the Reverend George Austen who sent a letter to the London publisher Thomas Cadell in 1797, introducing the "anonymous" work and comparing it to the work of popular novelist and Austen favorite Frances Burney. (The novel seems to have been promptly rejected.)

Jane Austen's father provides a marked contrast to the father characters in her novels, many of whom are negligent, weak, or, like *Northanger Abbey*'s General Tilney, outright villainous. General Tilney decides that the main character, Catherine Morland, isn't worthy of marrying into the family and kicks her out of the abbey at night. She is then forced to travel alone in the dark. General Tilney is also portrayed as a bore and remarkably obtuse, at first assuming wrongly—and hilariously—that Catherine is a wealthy heiress.

In *Northanger Abbey*'s General Tilney, Jane Austen presents a portrait of formidable power that is unopposed, as she will again with *Mansfield Park*'s Sir Thomas Bertram (more on that later). But she always presents an alternative: standing up to that power. Jane Austen, with her own father supporting her, writes about triumphs over bad parents. Despite being generally easygoing, Henry Tilney isn't intimidated by his father, and chooses to propose to Catherine without his approval.

LITERARY CONNECTIONS

In the very last lines of *Northanger Abbey,* the narrator raises the question of parental authority: "I leave it to be settled, by whomsoever it may concern, whether the tendency of this work be altogether to recommend parental tyranny, or reward filial disobedience." *Tyranny* and *disobedience* were weighted words in the late eighteenth century. In Henry Tilney's case, disobedience might win out.

Eighteenth-Century Boredom and Hints of Pride and Prejudice

In her last letters from Steventon throughout the year 1799, Jane Austen continued making acute observations and judgments—unlike those of the naïve heroine she was creating for *Northanger Abbey*. She also continued to suggest a growing boredom and disillusionment. But she also mentions another manuscript: *First Impressions*. Referring to the sisters' beloved friend, Martha Lloyd, Jane jokes that Cassandra best not show Martha this manuscript because "She is very cunning, but I see through her design;—she means to publish it from Memory, & one more perusal must enable her to do it." This early draft of *First Impressions* will eventually be published as one of her most acclaimed novels, *Pride and Prejudice*!

There's also a lot of sarcasm and joking in these last letters from Steventon. Included in her jokes are mentions of "the Miss Coopers," who are in fact imaginary. Jane writes of a cousin who has taken a "living" at a Staffordshire rectory and who she hopes to not hear from for fifteen years, when, she imagines, "the Miss Coopers are presented to us, fine, jolly, handsome, ignorant girls." The nonexistent Miss Coopers join a whole collection of made-up characters and situations Austen would joke about throughout her letters.

The shallowness of society that Austen wrote about in her letters made their way into different scenes in *Northanger Abbey,* where misinformation about novels, places, fortunes, and distances creates a lot of confusion for the main character (and for readers). The character of John Thorpe is the biggest purveyor of misinformation: he disparages Frances Burney's novel *Camilla* while actually describing a scene from Henry Fielding's *Tom Jones*. He also consistently exaggerates the speed of his horse, much to Catherine's disappointment. And his biggest instance of misinformation is the misinformation he gives about Catherine herself—that she stands to inherit a fortune from the Allens, which is false. This leads to villainous General Tilney's plotting. The truth will be part of the happily-ever-after in Northanger Abbey—and in all of Austen's novels.

The More You Know

Jane Austen's letters contain dozens of references to reading and to Georgian novels, including those by Frances Burney. Burney's *Evelina* is a favorite of Austen fans today. The miscommunication between heroine Evelina and the arrogant and powerful Lord Orville is a classic enemies-to-lovers plot that predates (and is thought to influence) *Pride and Prejudice.*

Bath, England

In 1801, Jane Austen, along with her parents and sister, moved from the parsonage in the Hampshire countryside to rented lodgings in Bath after her father retired. The move was sudden. In fact, Austen family lore has it that Jane fainted when she heard the news.

Bath was much different from Jane's rural home in the Hampshire countryside. A city of around forty thousand people at that time (compared to less than three hundred in Steventon), it was full of stone-paved streets, terraced houses, and ballrooms. Austen's letters following the move describe the Bath social scene as lacking pleasure or temptation. Almost as soon as the family had unpacked, Austen was recounting her experience with a series of "stupid parties" and transitory friendships in her new town. In her very first letter from Bath, the twenty-five-year-old Austen wrote Cassandra, "The first view of Bath in fine weather does not answer my expectations." The town itself she described in this letter as "vapour, shadow, smoke & confusion."

Such "shadow" and "confusion" permeate in *Northanger Abbey*, which Austen continued revising. In this novel, the fictional Catherine Morland, a kindhearted clergyman's daughter, travels with chaperones to Bath and makes her entry into society. At the town's Lower Rooms where society gathered, Catherine is plunged into "a mob" of diners and dancers but is left on the sidelines, since the rules of engagement depend on introductions by the master of ceremonies—the real-life master of ceremonies of Bath's Lower Rooms, Mr. James King.

But Catherine Morland—at first "imprisoned" on these margins of the crowded Bath social scene—eventually enjoys her time there because of a charming young man named Henry Tilney. At a crowded Bath ball where they meet, they exchange thoughts on novels, writing, duets, and Indian muslin. Suddenly Bath is a bit brighter for Catherine, and from then on, she searches for the reappearance of this Austen hero. Unlike Catherine Morland's, Jane Austen's search for fun and romance would continue in Bath without success. After her first recorded letter about the flirtations of Tom Lefroy, such a hero fails to appear in her surviving letters.

The More You Know

Regency-era conduct books insisted on clearly defined gender roles, while revolutionary writers of the time called for gender equality in education. In *Northanger Abbey*, Henry Tilney alludes to segregated education with his remark "Every body allows that the talent of writing agreeable letters is peculiarly female." Catherine argues, "I should not think the superiority was always on our side."

Out in Bath Society

Jane Austen was a reader of Hannah More, whose 1799 *Strictures on the Modern System of Female Education* urged young women to influence those around them through piety, leaving off balls, parties, and other "distractions." Austen's own novels would contain warnings and examples of how certain choices can impact someone's entire life. But she didn't maintain a sense of propriety alone where conduct was concerned; she also maintained a sense of humor, and didn't follow More's guidelines strictly. "I have a very good eye at an Adultress," she wrote to Cassandra while people watching at a ball in Bath. She was still settling in the city, and the family was apartment hunting at the time, but she had made the effort to dress "as well as [she] could" and was shown up to the Upper Rooms of the ball by her uncle and aunt. It was there that she observed this "adulteress" who remains elusive to history—but whom Jane found surprisingly commonplace, looking "rather quietly & contentedly silly than anything else."

While Austen herself didn't follow conduct books like More's *Strictures on the Modern System of Female Education* strictly, a character she was writing at the time did. She had hinted at writing *Pride and Prejudice* (then titled *First*

Impressions) in a previous letter to her sister, and through the character of Mary Bennet, she created someone who took the conduct books of her time to an extreme. Mary only speaks a handful of times in *Pride and Prejudice,* but when she does, it's to show the reader something about contemporary models of piety. She preaches even to clergymen, her seriousness contrasting with the humor and unconventionality of the other Bennet sisters. At a time when women were warned away from balls, dancing, and gossip, Jane Austen created a character that could outpreach any preacher.

The More You Know

In an 1809 letter, Jane Austen says when mentioning Hannah More's writing, "I do not like the Evangelicals." Later in life, however, she would write that the Evangelical approach to life might after all be "happiest & safest."

Dangerous Situations

In a letter dated January 25, 1801, Jane Austen wrote to Cassandra, "Your unfortunate sister was betrayed last Thursday into a situation of the utmost cruelty." The "cruelty" was a result of Jane's being stuck alone in the drawing room with a man "for ten minutes." Jane Austen is thought to be joking with her sister: The everydayness of "last Thursday" is trademark Austen, uniting the gothic with the commonplace for comic effect. And only a few lines up, Austen was asking her sister, "How do you like this cold weather?" But Jane continued that she considered sending for the housekeeper or Mary Corbett, a maidservant. Meanwhile "nothing could prevail on me to move two steps from the door, on the lock of which I kept one hand constantly fixed." It's possible that Austen did feel some danger.

The sense of both confinement and danger that Austen alluded to in her letter is deeply embedded in the gothic novels popular in the eighteenth century. One of the most famous is Ann Radcliffe's *The Mysteries of Udolpho*, which Austen's own hero Henry Tilney says he devoured in two days, "my hair standing on end the whole time." In *Northanger Abbey*, which is both a celebration and a send-up of the gothic novel, Austen traps her heroine in a carriage with the braggadocio John Thorpe, who refuses to stop so she can get out of the carriage. Even while granting readers the suspense and thrill of adventure sparked by a mysterious place and its possible perils, Austen maintains an ironic distance that encourages critical thinking about the art and psychological dimensions of gothic stories that Austen pays tribute to and also parodies.

LITERARY CONNECTIONS

Northanger Abbey is a novel about young people reading novels. Austen wrote it as a bold treatise on the novel as an art form worthy of being respected and celebrated. And in the pages of the novel she calls on other novelists to support each other, writing, "we are an injured body"—asserting that her own heroines would read novels unashamedly.

From Northanger Abbey, Chapter 5

Alas! If the heroine of one novel be not patronized by the heroine of another, from whom can she expect protection and regard? I cannot approve of it. Let us leave it to the reviewers to abuse such effusions of fancy at their leisure, and over every new novel to talk in threadbare strains of the trash with which the press now groans. Let us not desert one another; we are an injured body.

The Road from Manydown

One of the most appealing aspects of eighteenth-century life is the lost art of the house party. During this period, it was common for a household of the gentry to host a stream of guests coming, going, and staying for long dinners, cozy fires, country walks, games, and conversation. These house parties might involve a group of young people getting together and navigating social strategies, flirtations, and rivalries. Throughout her life, Jane Austen and her sister, Cassandra, themselves traveled across the country and lived as houseguests for weeks at a time.

One such party in 1802, at a time when Jane and Cassandra were mostly in transit, took place at the Bigg family's Hampshire estate of Manydown. Jane and Cassandra joined their friends, three sisters named Elizabeth, Alethea, and Catherine, at Manydown with their younger brother, named Harris Bigg-Wither. During the course of the evening, Harris even proposed to Jane, and she accepted! According to Austen biographer Claire Tomalin, the party rejoiced at this show of romance, which promised prosperity for Jane.

At the time, Harris stood to inherit the Manydown estate, and Jane was looking at a future as its mistress. The futures of Jane, Cassandra, and their parents were currently uncertain, and this alliance would put Jane in a position to provide them all with comfort and security and even to help her brothers make their way in life. But the very next morning, Jane retracted the engagement. According to Tomalin, Jane explained that "esteem and respect were not enough" and that accepting Harris would be wrong.

Jane rejected a large estate and the attendant power and influence it would bring. And she rejected stability at a time when she was displaced. At that house party at Manydown, Jane was—like the many heroines she would continue to write about—nonconforming, choosing instead to take a different path.

Literary Connections

Awful proposals make for iconic scenes in Jane Austen's novels. *Northanger Abbey*'s Catherine Morland is manipulated into a proposal she doesn't realize is happening. And Elizabeth Bennet rejects two proposals during the course of *Pride and Prejudice.* In Jane Austen's own life there's nothing to suggest her proposal from Harris Bigg-Wither was at all comical. Humor and irony in her fiction masks painful experiences, both in her novels and perhaps also in her life.

Two Letters

George and Cassandra Austen's move to Bath came after years of being rooted to a place where they tended to seven children as well as livestock and farm crops. From 1801 until the end of 1804, the family would move between lodgings in the city. But on a Sunday morning in January 1805, George Austen woke up at their lodging at Green Park Buildings having experienced fever and headaches the previous day. Jane was relieved that her father joined the family for breakfast and that he was able to walk without help. But by ten o'clock that night he was much worse, and by the next morning he had passed away. It was a sudden death for the family.

Jane sat down that same day to write a letter to her brother Frank—"Capt. Austen" at the HMS *Leopard*—letting him know of the "melancholy news" of their father's unexpected death. She mailed the letter, but another letter arrived the next day addressed from Frank to Cassandra; he was actually on his way to Portsmouth. So, Jane had to start over and write a second letter recounting the "melancholy news." The second time around Jane also mentioned that their father's latest illness was something "he had been subject to for the three last years." According to English curator and broadcaster Lucy Worsley, the lodging at Green Park Buildings was prone to flooding and damp, and might have caused George Austen's illness.

Austen scholars and fans alike believe that watching her father die in dank lodgings the family could barely afford inspired the themes of displacement and loss in her novels. Indeed, before *Sense and Sensibility* reaches fifty pages, Elinor Dashwood and her sister, Marianne, have experienced loss on multiple levels: They've lost a beloved father and an inheritance, and with their mother they've left their beloved estate of Norland to flee to a cottage in Devonshire. Then there is the ghostly presence of the late Mrs. Tilney, Henry and Eleanor's mother, in *Northanger Abbey*, and motherless daughters like Emma Woodhouse in *Emma* and Anne Elliot in *Persuasion*.

Literary Connections

The Austen family's experience of living in Bath, leading up to Reverend Austen's death (and after) was punctuated by disappointments in apartment hunting. Before the move in 1801, the family considered lodgings in the town's Axford Buildings, Queen Square, Laura Place, Charles Street, Sidney Gardens, Green Park Buildings, and Trim Street. Because the town is located on the River Avon, water and dampness was always a consideration when they looked for a place to live. The family's first lodging was found at No. 4 Sydney Place, but in the successive years the family moved to more affordable, and possibly damper, residences such as Green Park Buildings East.

New Lodgings

The death of George Austen left Mrs. Austen and daughters Cassandra and Jane in precarious circumstances, and they initially moved to a lodging at Gay Street and then to Trim Street, which Mrs. Austen apparently disliked, addressing one letter to a family friend as from "Trim Street Still." However, the sense of displacement wasn't new to the Austen family. As explored previously in this book, Jane's great-grandmother Elizabeth Austen was denied an inheritance as a widow and mother, and Jane's father was displaced as a child after the death of his father and a stepmother. On its surface the social world of nineteenth-century England seemed polite and orderly, but Jane was finding more and more that beneath that surface, things were a lot less stable and welcoming. Keeping a house and good social standing was difficult without a steady income.

The challenges of Jane Austen's world can be seen in the characters she would continue to write and refine, particularly *Sense and Sensibility*'s Elinor and Marianne Dashwood. These sisters are faced not only with difficult circumstances, but also with enemies: a brother who declines to provide them a share of their father's inheritance, and the malicious scheming of Lucy Steele, who knows Elinor has deep feelings for the hero, Edward Ferrars, but flaunts her secret engagement to him. The narrator makes Lucy's qualities clear: She combines "insincerity with ignorance" and also is "ignorant and illiterate." And that's not to mention the domineering mother and sister of the hero, the wealthy Mrs. Ferrars and Fanny, who try to stop Elinor from growing closer to Edward and who control who he marries.

Like Elinor Dashwood, Jane Austen was observing the people around her, dealing with loss, minding her manners, and gaining intel where she could. Like her heroines, she knew that these resources would help her navigate the world around her to find—if not love, like Elinor and Marianne—a sense of accomplishment, and maybe even happiness, through her writing.

Literary Connections

In her 1792 publication *A Vindication of the Rights of Woman*, which calls for equal education for women, political philosopher Mary Wollstonecraft describes the world that Elinor finds herself in. Here Wollstonecraft inventories eighteenth-century pitfalls for women, specifically the dangers of a sister-in-law: "But, when the brother marries, a probable circumstance, from being considered as the mistress of the family, she is viewed with averted looks as an intruder."

From Sense and Sensibility, Chapter 23

Supported by the conviction of having done nothing to merit her present unhappiness, and consoled by the belief that Edward had done nothing to forfeit her esteem, she thought she could even now, under the first smart of the heavy blow, command herself enough to guard every suspicion of the truth from her mother and sisters. And so well was she able to answer her own expectations, that when she joined them at dinner only two hours after she had first suffered the extinction of all her dearest hopes, no one would have supposed from the appearance of the sisters, that Elinor was mourning in secret over obstacles which must divide her for ever from the object of her love . . .

"Obstinate, Headstrong Girl"

Jane Austen's family were members of the gentry, and her mother's family had connections to English nobility. But the Austens worked hard to sustain themselves; especially after George Austen's death, the situation for Jane, Cassandra, and Mrs. Austen was unstable. After living in a couple of temporary lodgings in Bath, the three women moved in with Frank Austen's family in Southampton. They would stay here from July 1806 to July 1809, and Jane later wrote of her "happy feelings of Escape!" from Bath at this time.

Jane's letters to Cassandra over the next few months (while Cassandra visited their brother's estate at Godmersham) expressed her feelings about living life on the margins. In one letter, she described how the family entertained their family friend Captain Foote with an "underdone" leg of mutton, but Jane joked that "he was so good-humoured and pleasant that I did not much mind his being starved." Jane also updated Cassandra on their mother's spending habits—and Frank's—writing that "each party feels quite equal to our present expenses; but much increase of house-rent would not do for either." And she mentioned a nearby family, the Lances, reporting that they were "rich," and "we gave her" (Mrs. Lance) "to understand that we were far from being so; she will soon feel therefore that we are not worth her acquaintance."

The sense of social anxiety in Austen's letters sheds light on some of her fictional heroines—and sharpens the humor of certain moments in her novels, particularly when Elizabeth Bennet responds to Lady Catherine de Bourgh's questioning at the grand estate of Rosings in *Pride and Prejudice*. In their big confrontation at the end of the novel, Lady Catherine tries to intimidate Elizabeth into turning down any proposal from her nephew, Mr. Darcy. Lady Catherine's insults have become fan favorites, like: "Obstinate, headstrong girl!" But Elizabeth stands up to her despite the gap in their social status.

By the time of Rev. Austen's death and its resulting instability for the Austen women, the full manuscript for *Pride and Prejudice* had been written. However, it would take almost eight years before the world was finally introduced to an obstinate heroine who doesn't let her precarious circumstances prevent her from speaking her mind.

LITERARY CONNECTIONS

Despite the subversiveness found in Austen heroines like Elizabeth Bennet, an early reviewer, clergyman Richard Whately, the Archbishop of Dublin, wrote in 1821 that Jane Austen was "evidently a Christian writer." He added that because of her "good taste," religion in Austen's novels isn't "obtrusive. . . . In fact she is more sparing of it than would be thought desirable by some persons."

From Pride and Prejudice, Chapter 56

"If Mr. Darcy is neither by honour nor inclination confined to his cousin, why is not he to make another choice? And if I am that choice, why may not I accept him?"

"Because honour, decorum, prudence—nay, interest—forbid it. Yes, Miss Bennet, interest; for do not expect to be noticed by his family or friends, if you wilfully act against the inclinations of all. You will be censured, slighted, and despised, by everyone connected with him. Your alliance will be a disgrace; your name will never even be mentioned by any of us."

"These are heavy misfortunes," replied Elizabeth. "But the wife of Mr. Darcy must have such extraordinary sources of happiness necessarily attached to her situation, that she could, upon the whole, have no cause to repine."

"Obstinate, headstrong girl! I am ashamed of you!"

Grand Homes Fit for Heroines

On a summer day in 1806, just before setting up house in Southampton with her brother Frank's family, Jane Austen visited the ancient Stoneleigh Abbey. This Great House dated back to the twelfth century and was being handed down through Mrs. Austen's Leigh family at the time. Visiting Mrs. Austen's cousin, she and Jane found themselves sitting in the parlor of this grand place, enjoying "fish, venison, and all manner of good things," Mrs. Austen wrote to her daughter-in-law Mary.

In the letter, Mrs. Austen also described the grounds of Stoneleigh in a way that reminds some of Pemberley, Mansfield Park, and other key settings Jane was writing about: "The Avon runs near the house amidst Green Meadows, bounding [sic] by large and beautiful Woods, full of delightful Walks . . . " And not only that, when Mrs. Austen continued her epistolary tour inside the house, she described an upstairs apartment as having a "high, dark crimson velvet bed," and another bedchamber as "an alarming apartment, just fit for an heroine." Readers like Mrs. Austen and her family were devouring the new eighteenth-century art form known as the novel, with its grand houses, sublime settings, and gorgeous villains. Stoneleigh Abbey would have been the perfect backdrop for one of these novels!

Northanger Abbey's heroine, Catherine, dreams that Northanger will be like the grand estates she herself has read about, it doesn't impress her as much as Stoneleigh impressed the Austens. Northanger is described as being massive, like Stoneleigh, but it's decorated plainly and modernly by General Tilney. This villain had removed all the unique, gothic elements Catherine had expected—except for the shaped windows: "the pointed arch [of the windows] was preserved—the form of them was Gothic—they might be even casements—but every pane was so large, so clear, so light! To an imagination which had hoped for the smallest divisions, and the heaviest stone-work, for painted glass, dirt, and cobwebs, the difference was very distressing."

LITERARY CONNECTIONS

One early prototype for the alluring villains of Jane Austen such as *Northanger Abbey*'s General Tilney is John Milton's Satan in the 1667 epic poem *Paradise Lost*. This villain is eloquent, impressive, and—most of all—tempting for a naive heroine like Eve in the Garden of Eden. *Northanger Abbey*'s bad-tempered General Tilney—not to mention *Pride and Prejudice*'s intimidating Mr. Darcy—injects tension, and perhaps a sense of danger, into whatever room he's in. It's a quality to be wary of, in Milton or in Jane Austen.

Life after Death

The four years following the death of her father are thought to be the lowest point of Jane Austen's life, thanks to the instability of her income and lodging. First living in Bath, then in the port town of Southampton, neither of which Austen fell in love with, her letters at this time show that she carefully kept financial accounts, and dealt with the insecurity of lacking a father or a husband to provide stability in her life.

Six years would pass following her father's death before Austen would see a novel of her own published—and get paid for it. *Sense and Sensibility* would introduce the world to the character of Marianne Dashwood, who, very similar to Austen, experiences displacement and uncertainty after her father dies. But unlike Austen, whose letters reflect an embrace of reason and restraint, Marianne is a full-on romantic. She's a tall, gorgeous, emotional heroine who prefers the "picturesque," Romantic poetry, and unspoiled vistas. She doesn't worry about money or status and stays unsociably silent for the three days' carriage ride to London.

Marianne represents a romantic sensibility that views the world through a veil of rugged beauty: On a walk, she channels the lofty style of a Romantic poet, exclaiming about the leaves, "Oh! . . . with what transporting sensations have

I formerly seen them fall?" Elinor replies sardonically that not everyone "has your passion for dead leaves." And Austen shows that Edward is the perfect match for Elinor when he takes in the view and says, "I see a very dirty lane."

Marianne will nearly die of a broken heart. But in the end, she finds sufficient reason and restraint to join with her good fortune, her good looks, and her passions, and ultimately get her happily-ever-after. As wrong as Marianne might be at times in her all-out romanticism, she's also more courageous, more outspoken, more morally strong, and simply smarter than most of those around her, and is able to evolve over the course of the novel. Ultimately, the portrait of Marianne gives a sense that while she doesn't have much in common with sensible, wise Elinor, she does have more in common with Austen, who is always looking up to the one person who is smarter, wiser, and as ethical as she is: Her older sister, Cassandra.

LITERARY CONNECTIONS

Marianne Dashwood's taste in poetry reflects the poetry available to Jane Austen and her peers. Elinor says to her sister of John Willoughby, "You know what he thinks of Cowper and Scott; . . . and you have received every assurance of his admiring Pope no more than is proper." Austen, through Elinor, is able to play the critic here: William Cowper and Sir Walter Scott are known for intensity of feeling, Alexander Pope less so.

Settled in Southampton on a rainy day in February 1807, Jane wrote to Cassandra, filling her in on the dramas of neighbors and their mistresses, the delivery methods and costs of a gift of fish to bereaving friends, and the current blooms in her garden, namely the sweetbriar and "indifferent" roses, the currents, gooseberries, and raspberries.

But it soon became apparent there was someone else in the room where Jane wrote her letter. Jane described a "little Visitor," who was delighting her. This visitor was Kitty, the ten-year-old daughter of Captain Foote, a Royal Navy friend of Frank's, whom Frank has brought back with him from church that day. Kitty, Jane wrote, was "talking away at my side & examining the Treasures of my Writing-desk drawer;—very happy I believe;—not at all shy of course." Jane had anticipated her visit, and enjoyed it, perhaps for the company and also for the observations it allowed, as Jane mused to Cassandra, "What is become of all the Shyness in the World?"

Later that evening, Kitty had left, having become, Jane joked, her "very valuable friend." Jane admitted to Cassandra that what she observed in Kitty struck her as "so unlike anything that I was myself at her age, that I am often all astonishment & shame." A thirty-one-year-old Jane Austen, yet unpublished and unknown but about to become a successful author of novels with heroines like Elizabeth Bennet, was reflecting on her own youth, feeling ashamed of her shyness. In contrast, her protagonists would often be outgoing. Elizabeth Bennet would have a "lively, playful disposition, which delighted in any thing ridiculous." And Emma Woodhouse would have "a happy disposition" and a confidence that make her a successful socialite (in addition to her "comfortable home"). In Austen's novels, the world is a better place because of the impertinence of heroines who don't have the shyness she herself dealt with as a child.

LITERARY CONNECTIONS

Two characters in *Pride and Prejudice* appear to be painfully shy, and both belong to Mr. Darcy's prestigious family: Georgiana, Mr. Darcy's little sister, is nearly seduced by George Wickham, and Anne de Bourgh, Mr. Darcy's cousin and daughter of the powerful Lady Catherine, also seems to suffer from a shyness that prevents her from standing up for herself like Elizabeth Bennet does.

Aristocrats

The closest Jane Austen got to the life of her character Emma Woodhouse—enjoying leisure and independence on a grand estate "with very little to distress or vex her"—might have been in her visits to her brother Edward's grand estate of Godmersham. On a Wednesday in June 1808, Jane was sitting in the Yellow Room at Godmersham as she wrote to Cassandra. She'd been brought to the estate with a cold, and she recounted her arrival and her place there in detail to her sister: "Our two brothers were walking before the house as we approached, as natural as life." Their favorite niece, Fanny Knight, the daughter of the estate, came to see Jane "and stayed while [she] dressed." Throughout her 1808 letters from Godmersham, Austen observed the company around her, joked about being rich, and spent hours in her little "apartment" after breakfast.

But her letters also suggest that she was lonely, and dependent. She accepted her "usual Fee," thought to be some financial help from a family benefactor, Mrs. Catherine Knight (Edward Austen's adoptive mother), and she relied on her brothers to plan the logistics of her return home almost as soon as she arrived.

Throughout this time, Jane was able to observe and experience firsthand what life was like on a grand estate, but her primary experience seemed to be what it felt like to be on the margins of high society. Some classic scenes in Austen's novels involve members of the aristocracy—a Sir Thomas, a Sir Walter, or a Lady Catherine. But on closer view, few aristocrats are portrayed in a positive light in these novels.

In England at this time, the power base of the country was in the landowning, titled classes. Scholars note that Austen's inventory of awful aristocrats forces readers to examine power structures and who is fit to rule, whether the domain is a house, an estate, or a country.

LITERARY CONNECTIONS

Traditional readings of *Mansfield Park* have interpreted Sir Thomas Bertram as a benevolent landowner, a positive example of English power and order. But today, this character reads to scholars and Austen fans more like a benevolent dictator. His wealth is at least partly funded by an Antigua plantation; his advice leads his daughters to social and moral ruin; and he attempts to influence the heroine, Fanny Price, in a negative way, though she resists.

From Mansfield Park, Chapter 2

Fanny, whether near or from her cousins, whether in the schoolroom, the drawing-room, or the shrubbery, was equally forlorn, finding something to fear in every person and place. She was disheartened by Lady Bertram's silence, awed by Sir Thomas's grave looks, and quite overcome by Mrs. Norris's admonitions. Her elder cousins mortified her by reflections on her size, and abashed her by noticing her shyness: Miss Lee wondered at her ignorance, and the maid-servants sneered at her clothes; and when to these sorrows was added the idea of the brothers and sisters among whom she had always been important as playfellow, instructress, and nurse, the despondence that sunk her little heart was severe. The grandeur of the house astonished, but could not console her.

Aunt Jane

In the autumn of 1808, Jane wrote to Cassandra, who was staying at their brother Edward's Godmersham estate. Edward's wife, Elizabeth, had just given birth to their eleventh child. Jane wrote about her happiness and "great pleasure" to hear of the baby's arrival and the mother's "happy recovery," hoping "to hear of its' [sic] advancing in the same [sic] style."

Her letter continued with an update on her niece Fanny, the oldest child in the Godmersham household: "She is quite after one's own heart," Jane wrote, "give her my best Love, & tell her that I always think of her with pleasure." Like her character Anne Elliot in *Persuasion,* who longs for friendship and family and adores her nephews, Jane Austen was deeply attached to her nieces and nephews. She wrote about their interactions in her letters, expressing joy when they were affectionate. She also wrote about how they were developing, how they were doing if they were grieving, and more, all while providing guidance and fun. She played games with them, wrote poems for them, and shared in-jokes and letters with them.

But on an October Sunday just days after writing this letter, Jane had much more sobering family news to respond to: She learned from a letter from Cassandra that their sister-in-law Elizabeth had died. Jane wrote back from Southampton that "the sad news reached us last night." Elizabeth's death would leave Jane's brother Edward to raise eleven children, including Fanny. Jane wrote of the two older sons that she was "disappointed" they'd been sent from school in Winchester to Steventon to be with James's family after the death of Elizabeth, saying "I should have loved to have them with me at such a time."

However, eventually nephews George and Edward arrived in Southampton to stay with their aunt and their grandmother. Jane wrote about the fun she had with George and Edward during this time—of "spillikins, paper ships, riddles, conundrum, and cards" as well as strolling outdoors and rowing on the river. She had also started a card game called speculation with her nephews, and while she signed the letter by sending her "love to all," she joked that "we hardly knew how to leave off." She hoped to keep the boys in Southampton for as long as possible.

The More You Know

In her letters to her sister, Jane Austen vividly describes their nephews' activities: "While I write now," she says, "George is most industriously making and naming paper ships, at which he afterwards shoots with horse-chestnuts, brought from Steventon on purpose; and Edward equally intent over the 'Lake of Killarney,' twisting himself about in one of our great chairs."

Having Children in Nineteenth-Century England

The 1808 death of Jane Austen's sister-in-law, Elizabeth Knight, was noted solemnly and sympathetically around the neighborhood. Unfortunately, death from childbirth wasn't new to the Austen family. Over the course of their lives, Jane and Cassandra would lose three sisters-in-law to maternal mortality.

In October 1808, just before their sister-in-law Elizabeth died, Jane wrote from Southampton to Cassandra at Godmersham responding to some gossip from her sister about a woman named Mrs. Tilson: "—but poor Woman! how can she be honestly breeding again?" (According to Deirdre Le Faye, who compiled Jane Austen's letters, that last sentence was "canceled," or crossed out, by someone but remains legible.) Childbirth was rarely reported positively by Jane Austen, and she worried when her niece, Anna, started having children. She wrote to another niece, Fanny, of Anna: "Poor Animal! she will be worn out before she is thirty." In the very next sentence she continued, "Mrs. Clement too is in that way again. I am quite tired of so many Children." Austen herself would never have any children, but she did write about something with the pride and love of a mother: her novels. "I am never too busy to think of S&S," she wrote Cassandra, in 1809. "I can no more forget it, than a mother can forget her sucking child."

After her sister-in-law Elizabeth passed away, the cottage near Edward's Chawton estate was made available. And by July 1809, Jane Austen, along with her mother, sister, and close friend Martha Lloyd, were packing up their things in Southampton to move into the home, called Chawton Cottage. The move would put an end to roughly eight years of wandering, and Austen would soon settle into a life of comfort, stability, and inspiration. She was entering a period that would produce six published novels.

The More You Know

While only four of Jane Austen's surviving letters are to Martha Lloyd, it's clear how close Austen was to this friend. In their youth, they shared a bed and stayed up all night talking, and in July 1806, Jane wrote a poem voicing frustration at Martha being without an escort for a trip. Austen writes to an elusive escort for her friend, "Take her, & wonder at your luck, / In having such a Trust, / Her converse sensible & sweet / Will banish heat & dust."

Moving Once Again

In the spring of 1809, thirty-three-year-old Jane Austen was packing up once again to leave her lodgings at Castle Square, Southampton, for the cottage near Chawton estate. It had been nearly eight years of uncertainty. The years of wandering had started when she left Steventon with her parents in 1801 and moved to Bath. Things had become even more uncertain when her father passed away in 1805. Now Jane was again toting all her belongings, including her volumes of writings, sketches, and three full manuscripts (*First Impressions,* which would become *Pride and Prejudice*; *Elinor and Marianne,* which would become *Sense and Sensibility*; and *Susan,* which would become *Northanger Abbey*).

Other than her letters, Jane hadn't appeared to be writing much during these years of wandering—but she did have a draft manuscript of a dreary novel called *The Watsons.* The story was about the Watson family and heroine Emma Watson, who is educated separately from her sisters. It introduced themes of fortune, inheritance, money, status, and education that would come up in Austen's later novels. Eventually *The Watsons* was abandoned, although it's not known why.

However, before even arriving in the new home close to her brother's estate, Jane Austen got down to business:

The first letter of Austen's that survives from around this time was written to a publisher. There would also be letters from London, where Jane would embark on adventure—brimming with art and entertainment—all made possible by a renewed sense of place. At Chawton Cottage, Austen, her family, and her precious manuscripts would be kept safe and secure for the remainder of her life. Eight years of inspiration and creation were ahead of her! Still, wandering and a constant sense of uncertainty and displacement would continue to be a theme in every single story Jane Austen would tell. . . .

The More You Know

Jane Austen wrote of her "happy feelings of Escape" on leaving Bath, but the years in Southampton were possibly worse. After their father's death, the Austen brothers exchanged optimistic letters about their pooled financial contributions to their mother. However, the family record collected by Austen descendants and later expanded by Deirdre Le Faye says: "Jane was suddenly very depressed by the limitations of the life of her mother and herself by their bereavement and diminished income."

Mad at a Publisher

Among the items Jane Austen was moving with her to Chawton Cottage were the three unpublished manuscripts: for *Susan, Elinor and Marianne,* and *First Impressions*. The publisher Crosby & Co. had purchased her novel *Susan* (later published as *Northanger Abbey*) in 1803 for £10. Jane was just twenty-seven at the time, and Henry Austen's lawyer, Mr. William Seymour, had represented Jane and Henry (who was now helping to handle her publishing ventures) in the sale. The problem in 1809 was that after six years, the novel had still not been published.

So, on a spring day in Southampton as Jane was packing for her move, she wrote to Crosby & Co. The anonymous letter from "the authoress" of *Susan* (presumably, Crosby & Co. didn't know Jane's identity when they bought the novel) was short and businesslike. It reminded Crosby & Co. of the manuscript they had acquired and requested an explanation for why it hadn't been published. Jane also added that if "no notice be taken of this Address, I shall feel myself at liberty to secure the publication of my work, by applying elsewhere."

Mr. Richard Crosby's reply was swift and perfunctory: If Jane were to sell the manuscript somewhere else, he would "take proceedings to stop the sale." He did say that she could buy back the manuscript for the £10 the company had paid for it. Jane and Henry Austen were eventually able to buy back *Susan*. However, it wouldn't be published in Jane's lifetime; instead, it would be published posthumously, just months after her death in 1817, as *Northanger Abbey*.

To add a fine point to her frustration and disappointment in Crosby & Co., Jane had with sly wit in her letter jabbed the publishers with her signature—from a "Mrs. Ashton Dennis," the initials in the name spelling: MAD.

The More You Know

Within just a few years of her MAD letter, Jane Austen's writing would finally gain recognition, as her second novel, *Pride and Prejudice*, became the talk of the town. Two nieces, Louisa and Marianne, would look back on their time with their aunt, and recall that they frequently saw her writing what they thought were letters and that she would frequently "laugh to herself" while writing.

Chawton Cottage

By July 1809, Jane Austen had settled in Chawton Cottage with her mother, her sister, and a dear friend, Martha Lloyd. The Lloyds had been friends of the Austens since 1789 when the family came to live at nearby Deane Parsonage near Steventon, and Martha and Mary Lloyd, about twenty-three and eighteen at the time, became fast friends with Cassandra and Jane, who were sixteen and thirteen. In the spring of 1805, Mrs. Lloyd had died, leaving Martha on her own, and she began living with the Austen women. As they moved into Chawton, Austen was entering a period of eight years that would provide the stability she needed to focus on her writing. From Chawton House, Austen would write three new novels, revise the three she had previously written, and publish four.

Life at the cottage was reportedly comfortable, and Jane was hard at work on her novels during these more stable and secure years. In fact, *Sense and Sensibility* was bought on commission (Jane Austen, out of caution, reserved a small fund to cover any losses from the publication of this first novel) over the winter of 1810–1811, just a year after the move, by publisher Thomas Egerton. (Egerton would also publish *Pride and Prejudice* and *Mansfield Park.*) Austen was busy!

Letters from the first two years at Chawton have not survived; they pick up after a two-year gap in 1811, just before the publication of *Sense and Sensibility*, when Jane was thirty-five years old. But there's one exception to the silence of those early years at the cottage: a letter in the form of a poem, written in July 1809. Sharing verses was an Austen family tradition, and at the same time Jane was settling into her new home, she wrote this poem to celebrate the birth of her brother Frank's new baby boy. Her poem is full of affectionate jokes, wishing the new baby the same "insolence of spirit" as his father: "Fearless of danger, braving pain,/And threaten'd very oft in vain." She also assured her brother in this letter of "The many comforts that await/Our Chawton home—how much we find/Already in it, to our mind."

The comforts that awaited would help make possible the beloved novels Jane Austen would produce in the eight short years to follow—novels that continue to inspire centuries later.

The More You Know

According to family memories from Jane's niece, Caroline, the household routine at Chawton included Jane's beginning "her day with music," as well as making breakfast at nine o'clock: "that was her part of the household work." Jane looked after the tea, sugar, and wine. Cassandra looked after the rest of the food pantry, and Mrs. Austen enjoyed "Patchwork" and gardening while wearing "a round green smock like a labourer's."

Nine Notorious Years

One of the most tantalizing aspects of Jane Austen's novels is their setting: an era known in England as the Regency that has inspired an entire subgenre of romance novels. The Regency era technically spanned the nine years between 1811 and 1820 when the Prince Regent reigned in place of his father, George III, who was overtaken by mental illness. Although "the Regency" is often used more loosely to describe the late eighteenth century and early nineteenth century (around 1795–1837). The era's confluence of new political ideas, new artistic movements, and social unrest as well as innovation has made the Regency fertile ground for the imagination. While the wealthy few enjoyed it as a time of cultural refinement, increasing numbers were seeking Poor Relief from county parishes.

During an unsettling period of the Napoleonic Wars (1803–1815), revolutions in the American colonies and France, disputes about the global slave trade and England's role in it, and political conflicts in Britain's Houses of Parliament, the Regency was a time of vibrant—and destabilizing—debate. Radical politicians and artists like George Gordon, aka Lord Byron, and Percy Bysshe Shelley used their poetry and notoriety to call for justice.

The Regency era was also a violent period in England, with economic disparities and worker uprisings sometimes ending in violence by the state. A code of laws known as the Bloody Code brought the death penalty to more than two hundred infractions including petty theft. Meanwhile, women continued to have fewer rights than men. A married woman's property legally belonged to her husband, and it was almost impossible to get a divorce without an Act of Parliament (which meant getting the approval of the king!).

The More You Know

The Regency era in England was a time of injustice and protest: One of the largest protests of the era occurred in 1819 when thousands of pro-democracy demonstrators, including women and children, gathered in Manchester. The crowd met with a violent crackdown by authorities, injuring hundreds and killing about a dozen people. The incident, known as the Peterloo Massacre, became a symbol of tyranny in England, inspiring Percy Bysshe Shelley's poem "The Masque of Anarchy."

Regency Fashion

A red-spotted muslin gown. Bonnets sporting fake flowers. Pink shoes that are "not particularly beautiful." A kerseymere spencer jacket. A trusted brown silk pelisse. . . . These are all clothes worn and inventoried by Jane Austen in her letters, and later catalogued by historian Hilary Davidson in her book *Jane Austen's Wardrobe.*

The Regency was full of fashions—and fashion changes—and this didn't go unnoticed by Austen. She was fascinated by what people wore, and how fashion choices reflected a person's character. She was also interested in how those choices could serve as a way of expressing yourself, managing a budget, and having personal agency in your life—especially for Regency-era women, who experienced little agency. What Austen said about clothes in her letters might even act as a barometer for how connected and engaged she felt with the world around her at different times in her life.

It is thought that in her early letters, written from the security of the Steventon rectory, Jane's attitude toward fashion reflected more confidence: "I like the Gown very much & my Mother thinks it very ugly," she declared in October 1800. But in Bath, a city more densely populated and more status conscious, her fashion references might have reflected disillusionment: "You were right in supposing I wore my crape [sic] sleeves to the Concert," twenty-four-year-old Jane wrote Cassandra in April 1805, "on my head I wore my crape & flowers, but I do not think it looked particularly well."

Years later, settled at Chawton Cottage and visiting London just a few months before the release of her first novel, Jane was enjoying parties, walks, the theater, and socializing at Henry's London house as she wrote: "Miss Burton has made me a very pretty little Bonnet—& now nothing can satisfy me but I must have a straw hat. . . . I am really very shocking." It appears that the stability of life at Chawton, and her London adventures, were restoring an air of confidence and playfulness to Austen's letters.

In her letters, Jane Austen observed, judged, and engaged with fashion and the trends of her time. Like writing, conversing, and even marrying, fashion choices for Austen reflected how a person shows up for the world and any occasion, and tackles life's adventures.

The More You Know

A "true Indian muslin," as *Northanger Abbey*'s Henry Tilney described it, was a popular eighteenth-century fabric with a history. Also known as Dhaka muslin, it was a sought-after, miraculously soft weave made through a complex sixteen-part process. It used cotton that grew along India's Meghna River near Dhaka city, now Bangladesh.

A Regency Celebrity

As Jane Austen was crafting her stories and finding inspiration in this new era of Regency England, her reading included the poetry of the Romantics, a movement of writers who emphasized imagination, subjectivity, and an appreciation of nature. Rebelling against the social norms of the late eighteenth century, Romantics valued passion and beauty over reason and order.

One of the most well-known Romantic writers of Austen's time was poet, political radical, and free-lover George Gordon Byron—also known as Lord Byron. While Austen was still unknown, Byron was creating a brand for himself of a reckless, brilliant, and fatally attractive artist. Byron was notorious: He conducted a string of affairs with high-profile women, including Lady Caroline Lamb; his half-sister Augusta Leigh; and Claire Clairmont, the stepsister of Mary Shelley. Byron was also known to be bisexual, and seemed to have traveled to Europe to stay safe from authorities in England, where relations between men were outlawed and punishable by death. All of this made Byron a celebrity of the Regency era—and one that Jane Austen would have been well aware of. Eventually, Austen would even be published by Lord Byron's famous London publisher, John Murray.

Austen herself rarely refers to the Romantic poets like Byron directly in her letters, but in her novels, the themes of Romanticism—and its focus on rugged and wild nature, intense emotions, and art and poetry that celebrate extremes of natural beauty and feeling—are very much present in characters like *Sense and Sensibility*'s Marianne Dashwood and *Persuasion*'s Captain Benwick. Marianne must learn to adapt the intensity of feeling to a social reality that also incorporates the feelings and practical needs of others. Meanwhile, Captain Benwick indulges in his fierce sadness and emotional poetry while grieving the death of his fiancée—with heroine Anne Elliot warning him of the dangers of too much intensity, even in art. For Austen and Byron and all of the Romantics, the best use of imagination was to envision a better world—one that cuts through the hypocrisies and bloody codes of the era and allows for justice, liberty, and a pursuit of happiness.

LITERARY CONNECTIONS

As famous as Lord Byron was, not only Jane Austen but also two women in his own life overshadow his legacy: The first is his daughter Ada Lovelace, for her innovations in the field of mathematics. The second is Mary Shelley, the young wife of his friend, poet Percy Shelley. Byron, Percy, and Mary gathered near Lake Geneva one summer and challenged each other to write ghost stories. Mary began a tale that would become more famous than any of Byron's works: *Frankenstein*.

Willoughby Circles Back

Whatever Jane Austen herself thought of love, marriage, math, and money, *Sense and Sensibility* balances a sense of realism and what's necessary and possible in life with a strong belief that marriage should be based on genuine attraction and love. This was not always the prevailing view at the time Austen published Elinor and Marianne's story. Up until the eighteenth century and beyond, marriage and courtship for the upper classes were family affairs. Members of the aristocracy and the gentry often chose marriage partners from within their social and family circles, focusing on values like temperament, finances, social compatibility, and status. The eighteenth century was a period where pragmatism in the marriage market began to be overwritten by considerations for love and emotion.

Austen gave her very first published villain the fate of marrying without love and ending up only mildly unhappy. *Sense and Sensibility*'s Mr. John Willoughby is portrayed as gallant, well-mannered, and romantic, right down to his love for poetry and landscapes. He's also a heartbreaker who rejects Marianne, choosing to marry for money. What readers don't know until the story is almost finished is that he has been in love with Marianne all along. It all comes out on a dark and stormy night, when Willoughby travels to the Cleveland estate where Marianne has nearly died of a broken heart. Willoughby asks for Elinor's "forgiveness," and sends a message for Marianne: "Tell her . . . that at this moment she is dearer to me than ever." Willoughby admits his "false ideas of the necessity of riches," and Elinor notes that the "world had made him extravagant and vain."

While Willoughby hints that he can one day be with Marianne, Elinor informs him that Marianne will be moving on. And ultimately she does, finding love with Colonel Brandon. Willoughby's bad judgment in marrying for money instead of love, meanwhile, is something that Austen will continue to explore through her published novels.

LITERARY CONNECTIONS

In the spring of 1811 during a cycle of hot days and parties in London, Jane Austen wrote about *Sense and Sensibility* and "W's first appearance." The heartbreaking "W," Mr. John Willoughby, makes his appearance by Chapter 9 in the novel: As Marianne falls, he "put down his gun and ran to her assistance." Later, Willoughby "departed, to make himself still more interesting, in the midst of an heavy rain."

From Sense and Sensibility, Chapter 44

Elinor made no answer. Her thoughts were silently fixed on the irreparable injury which too early an independence and its consequent habits of idleness, dissipation, and luxury, had made in the mind, the character, the happiness, of a man who, to every advantage of person and talents, united a disposition naturally open and honest, and a feeling, affectionate temper. The world had made him extravagant and vain—Extravagance and vanity had made him cold-hearted and selfish.

Austen's First Publication

In the spring of 1812, *Sense and Sensibility* began to attract notice in the press. Reviews were published in *The British Critic* and *The Critical Review*, where the novel was called "highly pleasing, and interesting." It was also attracting gossip among readers in the aristocracy and the royal family! According to Deirdre Le Faye, quoting from a volume of Princess Charlotte's letters edited by A. Aspinall, the Prince Regent's sixteen-year-old daughter wrote in January 1812 of "Sence and Sencibility" that "Maryanne [sic] & me are very like in disposition."

Although the notoriously feisty princess found the novel relatable, it actually parodies the careless frivolity and luxury of the privileged classes. One iconic scene that captures this is when Mr. Robert Ferrars, the haughty younger brother of hero Edward, is at Mr. Gray's shop of London. At this jewelry shop, Robert painstakingly agonizes over which toothpick case he should buy. Also in the shop (and at first unnoticed by Robert) are Marianne and Elinor, who are exchanging some of their mother's jewels for badly needed cash. It's a clash of fortunes that isn't unnoticed by Elinor, especially when Robert finally does notice the sisters and looks at them with disdain.

Here, even haughty Robert Ferrars is no match for Marianne's own self-absorption, her own impatience with the world and its stupid details, and her own strong sense of superiority. Marianne is caught up in her own feelings, even as she's being judged by Robert: "Marianne was spared from the troublesome feelings of contempt and resentment . . . by remaining unconscious of it all; for she was as well able to collect her thoughts within herself, and be as ignorant of what was passing around her, in Mr. Gray's shop, as in her own bed-room." It's a scene that shows how the self-absorption, worldliness, and arrogance usually reserved for high-status men can be found in anyone, including a young, disenfranchised, and fiercely intelligent woman like Marianne.

The More You Know

Jane Austen has traditionally been associated with the conservative eighteenth-century philosopher Edmund Burke, who advocated for stability and order. But Austen's *Sense and Sensibility* and the difficulties of inheritance laws are compared to the philosophy of another eighteenth-century thinker: Thomas Paine. In his 1791 *Rights of Man*, Paine wrote, "Aristocracy has never more than one child. The rest are begotten to be devoured." The revolutionary Paine observed what Austen continuously illustrated in her novels: the challenges experienced by younger sons and children who do not stand to inherit land and wealth.

Paving the Way for Pride and Prejudice

The success of *Sense and Sensibility* allowed the publication of *Pride and Prejudice* to go forward, this time with publisher Egerton offering to buy the copyright for £110. When it was published months later, *Pride and Prejudice* would introduce Austen's second set of heroines and heroes to the world—livelier, bolder, and more problematic lovers than those in *Sense and Sensibility.* From their very first meeting at the Meryton ball, Elizabeth and Darcy face off: He's insulted her on his very first appearance, saying she is "not handsome enough" to tempt him to dance. And later, when the pair take to the dance floor, Elizabeth chides Darcy on his lack of social skills, telling him, "We are each of an unsocial, taciturn disposition, unwilling to speak . . ."

Scholars draw connections between the two characters and William Shakespeare's Beatrice and Benedick in *Much Ado About Nothing.* In fact, Austen may have drawn inspiration for her own writing from Shakespeare. She enjoyed the earlier author's works throughout her life, and the two stories have some key details in common, including a close-knit neighborhood of families and two people who seem smarter, livelier, and more disenchanted than everyone around them, yet dislike each other and make a show of it. Every time Beatrice and Benedick meet, there is a "skirmish of wits," and the same goes for Elizabeth and Darcy.

In both classics, the fun is not in the destination; it's in the journey. These enemies-to-lovers adventures take readers through obstacles, confusions, and misunderstandings to love and happily-ever-afters. These stories allow larger questions about society, class, marriage, money, and gender to be explored in a way that ultimately leads not only to community restoration but also to reconciliation and romance. As Benedick puts it to Beatrice after one final skirmish at their wedding: "Peace! I will stop your mouth." A rare-in-Shakespeare stage direction follows, and it's one that Jane Austen characters never indulged in her own writing: "[They kiss.]"

The More You Know

While characters never kiss in Jane Austen's novels, many Austen screen adaptations do end in kisses. In fact, Joe Wright's 2005 *Pride & Prejudice* had a new ending for United States and international audiences. Matthew Macfadyen's Mr. Darcy repeatedly kisses the face of Keira Knightley's Elizabeth. Apparently Wright, and possibly studio executives, thought Americans wanted more "sugar" and would care less about the film matching the novel.

A Disastrous Proposal

When *Pride and Prejudice* was first published anonymously, Jane Austen read the first half of it aloud after dinner with a Miss Benn, who was dining with the Austen family that evening. Their guest, Jane believed, was "unsuspecting" that Jane was the author. From this chance to re-encounter her own novel, Jane found Elizabeth's character "as delightful a creature as ever appeared in print," she wrote to Cassandra. But a few days later she wrote to her sister about a reading of the second half, again with Miss Benn present, but with Mrs. Austen reading, and now she has had "some fits of disgust"—she partly blames her mother's style of reading. She added that the novel was "too light & bright & sparkling:—it wants shade." (Austen scholars can only guess as to what she meant by "shade"—whether it was a less happy ending, heavier themes, or something else.)

While Jane Austen had her own critiques of her book, *Pride and Prejudice* emerged on the scene as an innovation. In the story, Elizabeth Bennet takes her "impertinence" further than heroines written before her, using both her feet and her voice to get out of precarious situations. She stands up to rakes and suitors and challenges authority figures like her own father, mother, and aunt-in-law-to-be, Lady Catherine.

In fact, Elizabeth Bennet's first big principled, forthright moment in the novel comes in her denial of Mr. Darcy the first time he proposes marriage to her.

In this scene, Mr. Darcy declares that he loves Elizabeth against his better judgment and in spite of her "inferior" connections. His presumption is followed by Elizabeth's refusal: "I had not known you a month before I felt that you were the last man in the world whom I could ever be prevailed on to marry." The conversation is closed—for now. But as readers were first discovering when the novel was published, Elizabeth and Darcy will eventually cross enemy lines and find a way to each other, navigating miscommunications, family politics, and pride and prejudices. They'll also arrive at what would become one of the most celebrated happily-ever-afters in literary history.

LITERARY CONNECTIONS

Modern enemies-to-lovers romance novels pick up where Elizabeth Bennet started in one of the sturdiest tropes of the romance genre. Casey McQuiston was inspired by Elizabeth and Darcy when writing her bestselling contemporary romance *Red, White & Royal Blue*. It explores issues of status, class, sexuality, and family in the romance of two privileged young men (with very powerful mothers) sparring and insulting their way to love.

From Pride and Prejudice, Chapter 34

"In vain have I struggled. It will not do. My feelings will not be repressed. You must allow me to tell you how ardently I admire and love you."

Elizabeth's astonishment was beyond expression. She stared, coloured, doubted, and was silent. This he considered sufficient encouragement, and the avowal of all that he felt and had long felt for her immediately followed. He spoke well; but there were feelings besides those of the heart to be detailed, and he was not more eloquent on the subject of tenderness than of pride. His sense of her inferiority, of its being a degradation, of the family obstacles which judgment had always opposed to inclination, were dwelt on with a warmth which seemed due to the consequence he was wounding, but was very unlikely to recommend his suit.

Regency Rakes

The Prince Regent, later George IV, was someone Jane Austen hated. Writing to Martha Lloyd in an 1813 letter, she said she "supports" the Prince Regent's wife, the estranged Caroline of Brunswick, "because she is a Woman and because I hate her Husband." However, Austen would dedicate *Emma* to the Prince Regent just two years later! This was most likely because he was reportedly a fan of her novels, and had requested the dedication.

The Prince Regent himself embodied many of the characteristics known as libertinism: a way of life that rejects, often out of assumptions of privilege, moral accountability or sexual restraints. And Jane Austen's novels are full of libertines, aka rakes—profligate, promiscuous, extravagant, and entitled men. Rakes are the kind of real-life villains who take advantage of those living on the margins. They use their charm to get what they want from the people (often women) who struggle to make a living or lack support or knowledge of the outside world. Anyone who was young, impressionable, or vulnerable was a target for the rakes of the Regency era and Austen's novels.

Examples of Austen's own rakes include Frank Churchill in *Emma*, and Mr. George Wickham, Mr. Darcy's nemesis in *Pride and Prejudice.* Frank Churchill especially is a true libertine: described as gorgeous, charming, irresistible, and ultimately superficial and dangerous. He almost drives Jane Fairfax into becoming a governess and ruining her chances of marriage and social standing; it's luck alone that lets them both have a happy ending. And Mr. Darcy saves Lydia Bennet from being an outcast in *Pride and Prejudice*—paying Mr. George Wickham to marry her after he seduced her into running away from her family.

The More You Know

For Jane Austen, the behavior of libertines was not just about moral conduct. It's thought that in her novels her larger point is about the power structures of the day. The novels question privilege based on land, inheritance, and wealth, and show its downsides for everybody else—a radical thing in the nineteenth century.

Lady Rakes

While Jane Austen's novels show both the attractions and the dangers of those privileged, unprincipled men of the Regency (aka rakes), they also show that a Regency woman could be just as rakish. In *Northanger Abbey*, Isabella Thorpe loves dancing and "horrid" novels, and readers often compare her to the rake Captain Tilney whom she runs away with. In *Mansfield Park*, the just-married Maria Bertram has an affair with Henry Crawford in London (an affair that makes the papers). Her sister Julia also makes a bid for Henry, and then elopes to avoid the consequences. Mary Crawford, meanwhile, jokes of "rears and vices" at the dinner table—shocking clergyman-to-be Edmund Bertram, who tries and fails to reform her in the novel.

Austen didn't need to look far for real-world inspiration for her female rakes. In fact, there were Regency women all around her whose entitlement allowed them to rake across the globe! There was Claire Clairmont, who followed her stepsister Mary Shelley to Lake Geneva in pursuit of her crush, Lord Byron (with whom she'd later have a daughter, Allegra). There was also Georgiana Cavendish, the Duchess of Devonshire, a friend and lover of the most powerful royals and political operatives of the Regency, who was thought to be pulling strings politically and in the royal court through these connections. But perhaps the most tantalizing rake of the Regency was Anne Lister, whose property and wealth allowed her the freedom to indulge in multiple affairs—one with her eventual wife, Ann Walker. Anne Lister's life of adventure and lesbian marriage is documented in her personal diaries. Originally written in a "code" using algebra and Greek, these diaries were discovered, decoded, and published in two volumes, in 1988 and 1992.

THE MORE YOU KNOW

Regency rake Anne Lister appears to have been conservative in many respects: She valued her privileged class and property-owning rights, and wanted to live and love within the institution of marriage, not outside it. So, on March 30, 1834, she and Ann Walker exchanged rings and vows and took communion together at Holy Trinity Church, in Goodramgate, Yorkshire, and afterward considered themselves married. The church displays a plaque commemorating their marriage. With her independence, her wealth and property, and her pursuit of adventure, the real-life Anne Lister is comparable to Austen heroes like Mr. Darcy.

Scandals in the Regency

For two centuries, critics and scholars of Austen have been tempted to see her as an author who observed and documented the polite, genteel, social world around her, with its rigid class hierarchy, its orderly manners, and its predictable rituals. But there were several diversions from this picture in Austen's own life—the international adventures of her cousin Eliza, for instance. And as she wrote her novels, Jane Austen also had the influence of one of the most celebrated and ridiculed lady rakes of the Regency: the Duchess of Devonshire.

Georgiana Cavendish, known as the Duchess of Devonshire, was married to the powerful Duke of Devonshire in 1774 at the age of seventeen, and they hosted royals and political operatives, strategized election campaigns, and maintained one of England's most powerful Whig families. But their life together was also full of unconventional arrangements and scandal. They had a polyamorous marriage, and Georgiana's best friend, Lady Elizabeth Foster, also known as Bess, was known to be the love of the Duke's life. In fact, the three of them lived together. Meanwhile, the love of Georgiana's life was an earl—Earl Charles Grey, of the bergamot tea family and fame. The unconventional couple also faced Georgiana's huge gambling debts and a hounding press.

The affections of a sister, Harriet Ponsonby, provide yet another key ingredient to the House of Devonshire: Also a gambler cohosting game tables with her sister, Harriet suffered through decades of an abusive marriage before finding the love of her life—the much-younger, dashing Granville Leveson-Gower, with whom she had two children outside of marriage.

Georgiana herself became pregnant with Earl Grey's child in 1791, and when the Duke found out, he banished her to France. She eventually renounced her love for the Earl in order to return to England and her place at Devonshire. Back in England, Georgiana took on a quieter routine, looking after her children, Bess's children, and the Duke until she passed away in 1806.

Georgiana's life is studied as a portrait of power, fashion, fame, and a troubled search for love that reflects the misadventures of Austen's heroines and the scandals they gossiped about and tried to avoid themselves.

LITERARY CONNECTIONS

Although none of Jane Austen's heroines are nobility themselves, her novels are full of regal titles. Among the nobility mentioned are Sir Walter Elliot, a baronet, in *Persuasion*; Sir Thomas in *Mansfield Park*; Lady Catherine de Bourgh, the widow of a knight and daughter of an earl, in *Pride and Prejudice*; and Lord Longtown, a marquis, in *Northanger Abbey*.

Inspiring Modern Romance Fiction

A common trope of romance fiction that often draws from the work of Jane Austen is a controversial one: the alpha male. This trope features a hero that is powerful, sometimes dangerous, sometimes wounded, and sometimes a combination. He's typically a complicated hero who resists love at first, then ultimately gives in. And many modern writers using this trope have found inspiration in *Pride and Prejudice*'s Mr. Darcy. In possession of vast lands, a massive estate, and £10,000 per year, Darcy is also shown to be arrogant, socially awkward, and nursing an injured pride. Yet he is unexpectedly smitten with the heroine, Elizabeth Bennet.

Shakespeare, who was one of Austen's favorite authors, created an early alpha male prototype in his *The Taming of the Shrew*. This character, Petruchio, is a domineering man who is confident he can "tame" the heroine, Katherine. In direct line of descent from Petruchio comes Austen's Mr. Darcy, who seems to be intimidating even to his friend Mr. Bingley—and just about everyone except Elizabeth Bennet.

Alpha males are usually men, but in contemporary romances, including those inspired by Austen's own stories, plenty of women or female-identifying and nonbinary characters take on this role, such as *Written in the Stars'* no-nonsense actuary, Darcy. And whether it's a contemporary Darcy or Austen's original character, the one thing every alpha male has in common is to come around, usually sweetly, articulately, and, to quote Mr. Darcy, "ardently" to the heroine. The alpha male trope is also about the lover on the other side of the equation: a partner who is worthy of a good fight, and who has a positive impact both on the alpha male and the world in general. The heroine and her love interest ultimately stand up for love and connection while conquering the obstacles society throws in their way, from class and wealth to their own inhibitions.

The More You Know

Jane Austen's heroines possess a deep appreciation for nature that extends beyond the manicured charm of English gardens. They are drawn to untamed landscapes and dramatic vistas, reflecting a broader aesthetic sensibility. Austen herself admired the eighteenth-century concept of the *picturesque*, popularized by artist William Gilpin, which encouraged a visually rich and emotionally engaging experience of the natural world. Austen's characters also respond to the emerging Romantic sensibility, which celebrated nature's power in all its rugged, unpredictable, and sublime beauty. Austen scholar Peter Knox-Shaw suggests that even the sudden, striking views Elizabeth encounters at Pemberley may reflect this untamed beauty.

From Pride and Prejudice, Chapter 4

Bingley was endeared to Darcy by the easiness, openness, and ductility of his temper, though no disposition could offer a greater contrast to his own, and though with his own he never appeared dissatisfied. On the strength of Darcy's regard, Bingley had the firmest reliance, and of his judgment the highest opinion. In understanding, Darcy was the superior. Bingley was by no means deficient; but Darcy was clever. He was at the same time haughty, reserved, and fastidious; and his manners, though well bred, were not inviting.

Dangerous Romance

Mr. Darcy may be one of the most beloved heroes in literary history to some, but others disagree. Some Austen scholars, critics, and readers see Mr. Darcy as literature's most alluring *monster*! They caution against the alpha male character and note the possible dangers of assuring audiences that such a man can be tamed or healed. Mr. Darcy protects Lydia Bennet when her family is at risk of becoming outcasts, but he could just as easily be their downfall.

Despite the critics, this mix of danger and seduction in a fictional character has evolved into other popular trends since Austen's time. That brooding, distant, impressive, and powerful hero is often a stand-in for fantasies about taming or conquering evil in horror-romance fiction. Heroes in these contemporary novels range from vampires and demons to actual monsters, like orcs and dragons. One example is Edward Cullen, the vampire hero of Stephenie Meyer's Twilight series. Edward is strong, aloof, and alluring. The heroine, Bella, can't stay away. And Edward himself shifts between being threatening and protecting Bella from other threats.

The display of power, protection, and hazard wrapped up in a hero like Mr. Darcy or Edward Cullen carries a potent emotional force. Beneath a surface of carefully constructed courtship rituals, these risky lover interests bring an undercurrent of danger and desire. Like legendary monsters, they belong to a scary world yet convey the magic of love. And like his vampire counterpart, Mr. Darcy is eternal. Because he's fictional, he's timeless.

Literary Connections

Romantasy, or romantic fantasy, is a popular subgenre of romance that brings the allure of world-building and the alpha male trope to contemporary romance and fantasy novels. Romantasy appeals to a generation that came of age during the Harry Potter and Twilight series, seeking stories with otherworldly heroes like vampires, werewolves, and fairy lords. Like an Austen novel, these fantasy romances are all about navigating the dangers of love and power.

Complicated Clergy

Everything known about the Austen family suggests that the clergy in Jane's own life—her father, the Reverend George Austen, and her brother Henry were more like her novels' heroes Edward and Edmund (aspiring clergymen from *Sense and Sensibility* and *Mansfield Park*, respectively) than the awkward Mr. Collins in *Pride and Prejudice*. While Mr. Collins shrinks back in horror when presented with a novel, Jane Austen's father and brother encouraged her in not only reading novels but also writing her own.

Additionally, Jane Austen was sharing a friendly correspondence with one of the most powerful clergymen in the Regency era: the Reverend James Stanier Clarke, the Prince Regent's librarian. Also a fan of novels, Clarke wrote a few fan letters to Austen in 1815, even asking her to create a clergyman character who, like himself, passed his time between the city and the country. Austen respectfully declined, explaining that she lacked the formal education to write such a character.

All these real-life relationships contradict how the clergy are often represented in the novels Jane was writing and publishing. Some Austen scholars believe this contrast reflects the controversy around novels in Austen's time: Some clergy supported writing and reading fiction, while others saw it as an indulgence that needed to be restricted. In *Pride and Prejudice*, when Mr. Collins arrives at Longbourn, the clergyman is invited to read a novel and recoils: "[H]e started back, and begging pardon, protested that he never read novels." Meanwhile the youngest Bennet daughters, Kitty and Lydia, "stared" and "gaped" at him, unaware that novels were forbidden. Mr. Collins then picks up "Fordyce's Sermons." James Fordyce's *Sermons to Young Women*, published in 1766, warns his young female audience of the dangers of fiction and of the "wit" that can ruin the paramount "ease" of a husband at home.

But like Jane Austen herself, her heroines are portrayed as intelligent and always looking to learn more. Some can hardly keep their nose out of a book, and others are witty in a way that disturbs the "ease" of male characters in certain situations.

The More You Know

The novelist and critic Rebecca West might have been among the first to designate Jane Austen as a feminist writer: In her 1932 preface to *Northanger Abbey*, West wrote that Austen's "feminism" was "marked" and "conscious." She thought it couldn't be a coincidence that right at the time of revolution in France, "a country gentlewoman should sit down and put the institutions of society regarding women through the most grueling criticism they have ever received."

An Austen Hero and Eighteenth-Century Enlightenment

As she busily wrote and published her works, Jane Austen was consistently exploring with many of her heroes (and villains) what makes a "good person." In his 1759 *The Theory of Moral Sentiments,* Enlightenment philosopher Adam Smith, who was also trying to determine this, described what he called the proud man. This person, Smith wrote, is proud for good reason, which makes him sincere. In Smith's theory, the proud man demands "no more of you than justice" and in fact he "disdains to court your esteem. He affects even to despise it." The proud man "seems to wish not so much to excite your esteem for *himself,* as to mortify that for *yourself.*"

Austen's Mr. Darcy reflects the traits of this "proud man." When they meet at the Meryton ball in *Pride and Prejudice,* Mr. Darcy insults Elizabeth when she overhears him telling Mr. Bingley that she is "tolerable; but not handsome enough to tempt *me.*" His character is shown to have the combination of pride, disdain, and fixation on justice that Smith wrote of his "proud man." When Elizabeth is told by her friend Charlotte Lucas that Darcy is proud but he has good reason to be,

Elizabeth retorts, "I could easily forgive *his* pride if he had not mortified *mine.*" Pride and mortification collide in Austen's novel, just as they do in Smith's philosophy. In another example, when Elizabeth later turns down Mr. Darcy's first proposal, a haughty, injured Darcy seeks "justice" and mortifies Elizabeth: "Did you expect me to rejoice in the inferiority of your relations?" Darcy responds with Smithian disdain and brutal honesty.

Lucky for Austen fans 250 years later, Smith also celebrates the Enlightenment virtues of sincerity, esteem, and affection. And fortunately for Elizabeth and Darcy, all that is on the way. . . .

LITERARY CONNECTIONS

The difference between actual goodness and the appearance of it are also themes of Jane Austen's and philosopher Adam Smith's works. Nature, as Smith wrote in *The Theory of Moral Sentiments,* gives people not only "a desire of being approved of" but also "a desire of being what ought to be approved of." This contrast is illustrated through opposing characters like *Emma*'s flighty Frank Churchill and the reliable Mr. George Knightley. Mr. Knightley tells Emma Woodhouse: "There is one thing, Emma, which a man can always do, if he chooses, and that is, his duty."

From Pride and Prejudice, Chapter 34

"And this," cried Darcy, as he walked with quick steps across the room, "is your opinion of me! This is the estimation in which you hold me! I thank you for explaining it so fully. My faults, according to this calculation, are heavy indeed! But, perhaps," added he, stopping in his walk, and turning towards her, "these offences might have been overlooked, had not your pride been hurt by my honest confession of the scruples that had long prevented my forming any serious design. These bitter accusations might have been suppressed, had I, with greater policy, concealed my struggles, and flattered you into the belief of my being impelled by unqualified, unalloyed inclination; by reason, by reflection, by everything. But disguise of every sort is my abhorrence. Nor am I ashamed of the feelings I related. They were natural and just. Could you expect me to rejoice in the inferiority of your connections?—to congratulate myself on the hope of relations whose condition in life is so decidedly beneath my own?"

The Economics of Austen

Jane Austen's writings show that she was very aware of the worth of things; her letters record the prices of gowns and stockings, pianofortes and music, as well as the salaries of curates, neighbors, and family members. She also wanted to make her *own* money, which she expressed explicitly in her letters. As she was getting down to the business of writing and selling novels at Chawton Cottage, she would write about the payments she received, or didn't receive, from publishers: "P. & P. is sold," she said to Martha Lloyd in a letter in 1812, "—Egerton gives £110 for it.—I would rather have had £150."

Her novels are also notoriously full of numbers: She calculates distances, annuities, interest, and incomes precisely, and the economics of life provide the backdrop for her novels from that famous first line of *Pride and Prejudice*: "It is a truth universally acknowledged, that a single man in possession of a good fortune, must be in want of a wife." But while she lays out financial details in her novels, she also transcends basic economies to portray another type of worth: a person's character or lack of it. The Middletons of *Sense and Sensibility* are wealthy landowners who are all about hunting (him) and children (her), and "these were their only resources." Resources, for Austen, are not only income but also character and integrity. The Middletons, with all their land, status, and wealth, have few inner resources. And in *Pride and Prejudice,* Austen upends Regency values when she shows that while Bingley's reported wealth wows those at the Meryton ball, his being a friendly person significantly boosts his value. Mr. Darcy, on the other hand, who is even more financially well-off, is devalued by those same ball-goers: "a most disagreeable, horrid man, not at all worth pleasing," says Mrs. Bennet of Mr. Darcy, equating value with character over money. Through misunderstandings, Mr. Darcy is seen by Elizabeth's family as being unworthy of her, despite how large his income is—"ten thousand [pounds] a year"! That is until he is able to clear things up. After getting engaged, he tells Elizabeth: "[H]ow insufficient were all my pretensions to please a woman worthy of being pleased." Austen again shows that true worthiness comes not from outer signs of status like financial means but from inner personal resources.

THE MORE YOU KNOW

In addition to Jane Austen's letters detailing finances, a record of the family's time at Chawton was kept by her friend Martha Lloyd. Called a "household book," it detailed recipes and rituals; keeping such records was a common practice in a Georgian household. From Martha, scholars know that the Austen household enjoyed pies and cakes, drinks of ginger beer, wine, and mead, and meals of vegetable pie, curry, and Jane's reputed favorite, toasted cheese.

Housing Security and Happily-Ever-After

While Jane Austen was shifting into more stable living conditions during her years at Chawton, she was still very aware of the issue of housing insecurity, as seen in both her letters and the novels she was writing. In the winter of 1813, Jane wrote a letter about her family friend Miss Benn, expressing anger at the landlord, "Old Philmore," who had evicted her: "Old Philmore is got pretty well, well enough to warn Miss Benn out of her House. His son is to come into it.—Poor Creature!—You may imagine how full of cares she must be, & how anxious all Chawton will feel to get her decently settled somewhere." *Pride and Prejudice* had just been published, and Austen was hard at work on *Mansfield Park*. In the next few months, she would also start writing *Emma*. In all these novels, she explores the vulnerability of living on the margins during the nineteenth century.

In her novels, Austen's happily-ever-afters always come with a piece of real estate—whether it's the merging of two family estates such as Hartfield and Donwell Abbey in *Emma*, or the grand grounds of Pemberley in *Pride and Prejudice*. In fact, as a Great House in England, Pemberley is not just a house: It's a tourist destination, a source of income, employment, and prestige. And like Austen, Elizabeth also deals with housing instability; since she has no brothers, her home will belong to a distant male relative when her father passes away.

Stuck in this insecure position in life, Elizabeth's eye is "instantly caught" by the view of Pemberley, a "large, handsome, stone building, standing well on rising ground, and backed by a ridge of high woody hill." In this moment, readers get not only a Romantic description of nature, but also a vision of home, family, and the stability of a place like Pemberley. In addition to the emotional resolution brought about by empathy, affection, and understanding between Elizabeth and Darcy, Pemberley offers a practical resolution, one that turns uncertainty and despair into stability and home.

LITERARY CONNECTIONS

Land in nineteenth-century England was the currency of power and wealth. In addition to his holdings from the Pemberley estate, Darcy receives an income from his own investments. Meanwhile, Mr. Bingley, whose total worth is "nearly an hundred thousand pounds," presently rents his home, to the dismay of his sisters.

From Pride and Prejudice, Chapter 43

Elizabeth, as they drove along, watched for the first appearance of Pemberley Woods with some perturbation; and when at length they turned in at the lodge, her spirits were in a high flutter.

The park was very large, and contained great variety of ground. They entered it in one of its lowest points, and drove for some time through a beautiful wood stretching over a wide extent.

Elizabeth's mind was too full for conversation, but she saw and admired every remarkable spot and point of view. They gradually ascended for half a mile, and then found themselves at the top of a considerable eminence, where the wood ceased, and the eye was instantly caught by Pemberley House, situated on the opposite side of the valley, into which the road with some abruptness wound. It was a large, handsome stone building, standing well on rising ground, and backed by a ridge of high woody hills; and in front a stream of some natural importance was swelled into greater, but without any artificial appearance. Its banks were neither formal nor falsely adorned. Elizabeth was delighted.

Adventure and Bargain Hunting in London

Jane's first known letter to Cassandra from her years at Chawton came not from her cottage home but from London. In the spring of 1811, she made an extended visit to her brother Henry's London house. Her letters during this visit are full of talk of socializing, art, and creative pursuits. In these letters, she detailed a party being planned by Henry and his wife, Eliza, with an invitation list of eighty guests. She also visited museums with Henry and Eliza, and said it was a competition to know where to look when at such places, since she preferred people watching and real-life "Men & Women" to pictures. Her people watching included acquaintances from Continental Europe, and she noted, "It will be amusing to see the ways of a French circle."

Jane was also bargain hunting: She walked to Grafton House and battled "thronged" counters and crowds to purchase bugle trimming and three pairs of silk stockings for less than 12 shillings a pair. Additionally, she was excited by the theater, attempting (but failing) to catch a performance by the popular actress Sarah Siddons. This letter showed a lift in spirits compared with her time living in Southampton and Bath:

"I find all these little parties very pleasant," Jane wrote, in contrast to the "stupid parties" she had described before, and the more melancholy tone of her Southampton and Bath letters.

And in the midst of her London adventures, Jane's letters answered a question from Cassandra about a manuscript successfully placed with a publisher: the manuscript published as *Sense and Sensibility*. It's a rare mention of her writing process in a letter, and she was pleased with how things were going: "I am never too busy to think of S&S," she wrote. She was correcting proof "sheets" of the novel (referring to the duodecimo format of printed books at the time; one "sheet" was folded to make twelve leaves, which equaled twenty-four total pages of a book), and after years of conjuring worlds, characters, and situations, her very first published novel was about to make its appearance in the world. Jane Austen was now thirty-five, and her letters showed her to be filled with inspiration and joy.

LITERARY CONNECTIONS

The business of publishing is mentioned more often in Jane Austen's letters than is her writing process. "You will be glad to hear that every Copy of S&S is sold," she wrote in July 1813 to her brother Francis. She added, "I have now therefore written myself into £250.—which only makes me long for more." (At that time, a decent annual income to live just comfortably, with no luxuries, was about £500.)

Writing Mansfield Park

By February of 1813, Jane Austen had spent nearly two years tending the house, garden, and her manuscripts at Chawton. She had now seen two of these manuscripts published, *Sense and Sensibility* and *Pride and Prejudice*. A letter to her sister also gives insight into a new project Austen was working on—something she called "a complete change of subject," saying: "Now I will try to write of something else." This "something else" refers to research she was conducting for her next novel, *Mansfield Park*. Sometimes cited by Austen readers as their least favorite, this novel takes a bit of a turn from her previous stories. Considered darker and more introspective than her other works, *Mansfield Park* is a study of power. And one major source of power for a young person in the Regency that Austen always explored in her novels was parents. The parents in *Mansfield Park*, Sir Thomas and Lady Bertram, are thought to be the most awful in all of Austen.

By the summer of 1813, a thirty-seven-year-old Jane Austen was witnessing parenthood (or a lack of it) firsthand as she wrote *Mansfield Park*. She spent a lot of time with her many nieces and nephews during this time, including a month's visit with nieces Cassy and Harriet at Chawton Cottage. Writing to Frank about the stay, she said she was sorry to see them go, but that in her brother and sister-in-law's parenting of the girls, "Method has been wanting." For Austen, parenting was a process of training and education, and one to be taken seriously—even for girls.

Coming of age is hard work in Austen's novels, but she shows that in the absence of trustworthy, stable parenting, a person can still educate themselves and attract love and friendship. If all else is lost, a heroine or hero can rally their own resources and develop a "Method" to get them by.

Literary Connections

A January 1813 letter to Cassandra gives insights about Austen's writing process and her view of her readers. She mentions lopping and cropping the new *Pride and Prejudice*, calls the character of Elizabeth "delightful," and muses on whether a "said he" or a "said she" might have made the dialogue clearer. However, she goes on, "I do not write for such dull Elves." The reference borrows a line from Sir Walter Scott's poem "Marmion": "I do not write for that dull elf / Who cannot image to himself." Austen felt that her readers were sharp enough to use their imaginations.

Horrid Aunts

When Jane Austen sat down to finish writing the something "entirely different" (*Mansfield Park*) in 1813, *Pride and Prejudice* was hitting the shelves and circulating libraries, *Sense and Sensibility* was headed for a second printing, and *Northanger Abbey* was still waiting for its debut. Settled and working from Chawton, thirty-seven-year-old Austen was writing a novel that's still as misunderstood, debated, and sometimes even ignored by readers as it was when first published.

Mansfield Park is a coming-of-age tale about an impoverished ten-year-old girl arriving to live on a grand estate with her wealthy relations. The novel reveals that, at the time she was writing it, Austen saw deeply into the strictures placed on a young person during her lifetime. Here, the parade of awful aristocrats and parents depicted with humor in her early writings and first novels take on an air of "guilt and misery" (even as the narrator promises not to dwell on such things!). Softening her usual ironic, distanced tone, Austen becomes more strident in this novel, portraying extremes of goodness and evil.

Heroine Fanny Price is perfect, to the point of distraction; she has such high moral standards for herself and everyone else that it can frustrate readers. She represents Goodness. Meanwhile, her two aunts at Mansfield represent extremes of Badness: Lady Bertram is depicted as a very passive person who doesn't "think deeply," and Aunt Norris as a domineering, self-righteous character who has "never been kind" to Fanny. It's through Aunt Norris's lecturing in particular that readers are shown the difficulties a young, marginalized person like Fanny faces in navigating the world. Ultimately, Fanny will use her intelligence, self-command, and goodness to win love, affection, and housing stability, like all Austen heroines do—despite the high stakes, and powerful odds against her.

LITERARY CONNECTIONS

Fanny Price is compared to another literary heroine: Cinderella. Both characters are good, respectful young women who are treated badly by the wealthy relatives they are forced to live with (Fanny by Aunt Norris and Lady Bertram, and Cinderella by her stepmother and stepsisters). And both characters are rewarded their "prince" by the end of the story—Fanny marries Edmund Bertram and Cinderella marries Prince Charming.

One Sensible Mother

As Jane Austen was setting a serious tone for *Mansfield Park*, her letters were also becoming less playful and amusing, particularly when it came to her mother. "I am very grand indeed," a twenty-two-year-old Jane Austen had written to Cassandra in the Steventon days, "—I had the dignity of dropping out my mother's Laudanum last night." A mixture of opium and alcohol, laudanum was used commonly in English households throughout the eighteenth and nineteenth centuries, and into the early twentieth century. It was prescribed for everything from menstrual pain and coughing to insomnia. Taken by adults and even infants, it was seen as a "cure-all" until people better understood its addictive qualities. Austen mentioned her mother using laudanum in multiple letters to her sister, and alluded to Mrs. Austen's bad health as well. In one letter, Austen wrote that their mother "has a very dreadful cold in her head," then went on to say that she herself had "not much compassion for colds in the head." Her mentions of her mother had become less sympathetic over the years.

Meanwhile, as she was writing *Mansfield Park*, she was creating a mother figure, Lady Bertram, who spends her days reclining on a sofa with her pug and deferring to Aunt

Norris's judgments about everything. By contrast, in her first novel, *Northanger Abbey*, Austen presented the heroine's mother, Mrs. Morland, as an antidote to the gothic evil and "romantic alarm" of the book, insisting on what's known and of real value (gratitude for family, home, and friendships). After a visit to family friends, Mrs. Morland encourages the evicted and dejected Catherine to consider "the happiness of having such steady well-wishers as Mr. and Mrs. Allen, and the very little consideration which the neglect or unkindness of slight acquaintance like the Tilneys ought to have with her," relegating the villainous General Tilney to the category of "slight" and insignificant.

THE MORE YOU KNOW

Patricia Rozema's 1999 film, *Mansfield Park*, is one of the only Austen adaptations directed by a woman. It features a performance by Lindsay Duncan that interprets the character of Lady Bertram, the mistress of Mansfield Park, as a laudanum addict. In addition to the theme of addiction, Rozema's *Mansfield Park* is also one of the only adaptations that openly alludes to slavery.

From Mansfield Park, Chapter 2

To the education of her daughters Lady Bertram paid not the smallest attention. She had not time for such cares. She was a woman who spent her days in sitting, nicely dressed, on a sofa, doing some long piece of needlework, of little use and no beauty, thinking more of her pug than her children, but very indulgent to the latter when it did not put herself to inconvenience, guided in everything important by Sir Thomas, and in smaller concerns by her sister. Had she possessed greater leisure for the service of her girls, she would probably have supposed it unnecessary, for they were under the care of a governess, with proper masters, and could want nothing more. As for Fanny's being stupid at learning, "she could only say it was very unlucky, but some people *were* stupid, and Fanny must take more pains: she did not know what else was to be done; and, except her being so dull, she must add she saw no harm in the poor little thing, and always found her very handy and quick in carrying messages, and fetching what she wanted."

"Dead Silence" and Abolitionist Themes

The grand estate of *Mansfield Park* is beautiful, especially as seen through the eyes of Fanny Price after she has been banished and then returned: "Her eye fell every where [sic] on lawns and plantations of the freshest green; and the trees, though not fully clothed, were in that delightful state, when farther beauty is known to be at hand, and when, while much is actually given to the sight, more yet remains for the imagination."

But taking a look below the surface of these bucolic grounds, many details reveal that the estate is financed by a plantation worked by enslaved people in Antigua. This means Mansfield Park benefits from the slave trade, which had been banned by the Slave Trade Act of 1807. The act didn't end the debates in Britain on the issue, though, and would have impacted the financial stability of Sir Thomas's estates. The background issue of the slave trade comes to the forefront of this novel in a scene that takes place at the dinner table of the estate, when patriarch Sir Thomas, Fanny's uncle, has just returned from a trip from Antigua. Fanny, describing the scene later to Edmund Bertram, says she'd brought up the question of the slave trade to her uncle, and it was met by the dinner party with "dead silence."

When Austen was writing *Mansfield Park,* many writers had been tackling issues of race, power, and oppression, from Olaudah Equiano to Austen's favorite, Thomas Clarkson. And in the background were many Black lives of the Georgian era that were increasingly getting the spotlight, including the composer Ignatius Sancho and Dido Elizabeth Belle—and thousands of others. Their lives are not represented on the pages of *Mansfield Park,* but in the centuries since, scholars and readers have been reading between the lines of Austen's novels. At the center of *Mansfield Park* is a shy child whose experience of marginalization in a grand space is thought to reflect oppression, immorality, and the abuse of power in the real world.

The More You Know

The Mansfield Park property isn't alone: In 2020, the UK's National Trust, which preserves hundreds of historic Great Houses, castles, parks, and collections, released a 115-page report finding that nearly a third of its properties were directly linked to colonial histories or the slave trade. It's "not that surprising," the report said, since "the practice of enslaving African people was a fundamental part of the British economy in the late seventeenth, eighteenth and early nineteenth centuries."

Two Cousins and a Portrait for the Ages

For many who know the story of writer Dido Elizabeth Belle, Fanny Price—the heroine of *Mansfield Park*—rings a familiar bell. Dido Elizabeth Belle was born in 1761, just fourteen years before Jane Austen, and then died thirteen years before Austen, in 1804. Born to Maria Bell, who is believed to have been formerly enslaved, and Sir John Lindsay, a white navy captain, Belle was raised for much of her life at Kenwood House, the estate of her paternal great-uncle, the Lord Chief Justice William Murray, Lord Mansfield.

Evidence suggests that Dido Belle was brought up at Lord Mansfield's Kenwood estate as part of the family and alongside her white cousin named Lady Elizabeth Murray, who was also a grand-niece of Lord Mansfield. According to the conservation nonprofit English Heritage, Belle was accomplished in music, languages, and etiquette, and may have played a vital role in the grand house, looking after the chicken and poultry yards at Kenwood, and caring for her uncle as he aged. A snapshot from Belle's life at Kenwood was captured in a circa-1776 painting (possibly by artist David Martin, but the source is disputed). The painting portrays

Elizabeth Murray, her arm outstretched to her companion, a fashionably dressed Dido with her finger coyly posed on her cheek in a playful pose. It's a picture that evokes harmony and sisterhood in a world that is complicated, both in and beyond the boundaries of a grand English estate—a vision of harmony that *Mansfield Park* and its inhabitants fail to achieve.

The More You Know

Not only does Dido Elizabeth Belle's great-uncle share a title—Lord Mansfield—with the Jane Austen novel having as a backdrop the African slave trade; Lord Mansfield also decided several impactful cases on the legality of the slave trade while his grand-niece was being raised on his estate. For example, he ruled in the 1772 Somerset case that the enslaved James Somerset could not be forcibly transported from England by slaveowner Charles Stewart. His ruling was a major event in England and America, paving the way for the official outlaw of the British slave trade in 1807.

Fanny Price, Monster

On an autumn day in 1813, Jane Austen was at her brother Edward's estate of Godmersham. In a letter to Cassandra, she wrote: "I am now alone in the library, Mistress of all I survey," and in a letter a couple days later to her brother Frank she joked about the "happy Indifference of East Kent wealth." The library was expansive: On the south wall, one shelf alone contained influential eighteenth-century works by William Gilpin on the picturesque, Edmund Burke's *Reflections on the Revolution in France*, and volumes of travel writing chronicling trips through Britain, Europe, Africa, and Asia. During her visit to Godmersham and its grand library, Jane was busy writing *Mansfield Park*, creating the character of a young, uneducated girl who develops into a great reader and thinker.

As Austen herself did, Fanny Price feeds off and grows from the advantages that surround her, yet she remains an outsider. Arriving at Mansfield Park at just ten years old, Fanny cries, is awkward, and pines for her cousin Edmund. All this makes her Jane Austen's least-loved heroine by fans. The late critic Nina Auerbach also wouldn't help Fanny's image when, in a 1980 essay, she compared Fanny Price to Frankenstein's monster. She wrote that Price "is unconvivial, a spoiler of ceremonies. . . . She exists like Mary Shelley's *Frankenstein* as a silent censorious pall."

Fanny is a girl on her own in the world, regularly bursting into tears and unable to find Europe on a map. However, Fanny grows tall, elegant, and brilliant as the story goes on—by the end of the novel she's admired by not only Henry Crawford but also by her uncle. A ball is given in her honor, and she has become Edmund's most respected confidant. And Fanny Price achieves what was often elusive for Austen herself: wealth, romance, and marriage. But as the "monster" slaying Mansfield, Price also stands up to abusive power and privilege. And she triumphs.

LITERARY CONNECTIONS

Fanny Price's reading list is extensive. It includes a volume documenting Lord Macartney's voyage to China, which, as researcher Azar Hussain points out, in the Jane Austen Society of North America's *Persuasions On-Line,* was serialized in *The Lady's Magazine* that Jane Austen might have read.

Sinister Siblings

Jane Austen's letters reflect her relationships with her siblings: With Cassandra, she was cheerful and deferential as well as confiding and loving; with her older brothers, she was ironic (at least, as she described in her letters to her sister); and with Henry, she was also loving and bemused, as he worked his way through a series of professions, charming people wherever he went. At one point, Jane exclaimed of Henry to Cassandra: "Oh! what a Henry." (In typical Austen fashion, the comment is a bit cryptic, but can be interpreted as referring to Henry as charming, energetic, and unpredictable.)

The dynamism and theatrics of her own siblings, who were decidedly nicer, nevertheless influenced Austen's imagination as she was creating the sibling relationships in *Mansfield Park.* In her novel, these charismatic, if mesmerizingly awful, characters flirt and scheme as Fanny watches in horror and fascination. The sibling cast includes Julia and Maria Bertram, the entitled Bertram sisters who are encouraged by their Aunt Norris in their superiority to cousin Fanny, and their oldest brother, Tom Bertram, the drunken heir to Mansfield Park. And then there are Henry and Mary Crawford; not only are these two diabolical siblings trying to seduce

Fanny and Edmund, the younger Bertram brother, but they also openly inform each other of their exploits and abet each other's attempted seductions. In fact, Henry and Mary—and the Bertram sisters—are shown as operating with a different moral code than Fanny Price and Edmund Bertram.

The two cousins have a front-row seat for each other's lessons in love—and they learn from each other's mistakes and triumphs, much like Jane Austen must have learned from her siblings. For the Crawford siblings, they are learning the hard way, if at all, about what happens when someone follows desire in the form of sexual gratification, land, wealth, and status . . . even at the cost of integrity, virtue, and true affection. Ultimately in the characters of Edmund and Fanny, Austen allowed young readers to escape from the temptations of not only the Crawfords but materialistic English values in general.

LITERARY CONNECTIONS

In a famous essay on Jane Austen, British modernist writer Virginia Woolf contemplated that a fifteen-year-old Jane Austen started writing mostly to make her siblings laugh. But at some point, Woolf wrote, genius took over and Austen became a serious writer: She "was writing for everybody, for nobody, for our age, for her own."

Mary's Harp and Fanny's Chain

Jane Austen wasn't just shifting the tone of her writing as she worked on *Mansfield Park*; some believe this novel also offers something not commonly found in novels during her time: LGBTQIA+ themes. Amid all the theatrics of *Mansfield Park*, a unique alliance is struck between the alluring Mary Crawford and the innocent and demure Fanny Price. Throughout the novel, Fanny has been growing in intelligence, character, and elegance alongside the worldly, confident Mary. The two have developed a relationship largely through sauntering "about together many an half hour in Mrs. Grant's shrubbery."

Despite all the sauntering, Austen doesn't base this friendship on a connection in spirit, intellect, or circumstance; there's something else that "seemed a kind of fascination" to Fanny. This something else is what scholars like Jade Higa might call the queering of Jane Austen (specifically, in Higa's words, "queer possibilities"), or a shift from the heteronormative structures other novels often follow. This theory comes from critical study by Higa and others, exploring the in-between spaces of romance and friendship. In an essay in the collection *Jane Austen, Sex, and Romance*, Higa highlights scenes between Mary and Fanny that involve Mary's alluring harp playing and a particularly intimate scene where Mary stands in to woo for her brother, tempting a reluctant Fanny into accepting a gold chain to wear to a ball. Mary's offer makes "Fanny start back at first with a look of horror," but eventually Fanny accepts, saying, "When I wear this necklace I shall always think of you." It's argued that through *Mansfield Park*, Austen is exploring relationships outside the expected constructs and allowing characters to love outside the strictures of their society. It's a possibility Higa calls "an embrace of the nonnormative, the potentially messy, and the beautifully complex." Relationships in the pages of Austen, and particularly in *Mansfield Park*, veer away from the familiar pathways of her own world to explore affections, connections, and desire in unique ways.

LITERARY CONNECTIONS

Jane Austen scholar Clara Tuite talks about the queering of Jane Austen in her book *Romantic Austen: Sexual Politics and the Literary Canon*. Here, Tuite argues that Austen has become a figure of queer attachment—both in terms of her readers' relationships to her work and in reinterpretations of her characters and plots. As she explains, Austen's novels and persona are taken up in fan cultures, academic spaces, and popular media as tools to explore diverse desires and identities.

From Mansfield Park, Chapter 22

"This is pretty, very pretty," said Fanny, looking around her as they were thus sitting together one day; "every time I come into this shrubbery I am more struck with its growth and beauty. Three years ago, this was nothing but a rough hedgerow along the upper side of the field, never thought of as anything, or capable of becoming anything; and now it is converted into a walk, and it would be difficult to say whether most valuable as a convenience or an ornament; and perhaps, in another three years, we may be forgetting—almost forgetting what it was before. How wonderful, how very wonderful the operations of time, and the changes of the human mind!"

"Fancy Me"

Jane Austen stayed at her brother Edward's Great House, Godmersham, throughout the autumn of 1813, enjoying all the comings and goings and parties and balls. But according to her letters at the time, she was happy to skip a ball in favor of a day in Godmersham's grand library. One morning before breakfast she began a letter to Cassandra saying she was "very snug, in my own room . . . excellent fire, fancy me." But sometimes she and Edward's family had exciting visitors: "[Y]esterday Fanny & I sat down to breakfast," she writes, "with six gentlemen to admire us."

During this Godmersham autumn of socializing and ease, Austen was living in a world that looked like the one of her next published novel, *Mansfield Park*. Like Austen, *Mansfield Park*'s heroine, Fanny Price, is surrounded by the society and family of a grand house, but while Austen suggested that she was having a good time during her stay, Fanny is shown to be very much alone. Having left her poor, struggling family for Mansfield Park when she was just ten years old, Fanny is often seen as a precursor to the iconic orphans of literature to come, from Charles Dickens's Oliver Twist and David Copperfield, to Charlotte Brontë's Jane Eyre. And Austen herself encountered literary orphans who may have inspired Price, from Shakespeare's twins Viola and Sebastian, to Samuel Richardson's Harriet Byron and Henry Fielding's Tom Jones.

Soon after the Godmersham autumn of 1813, Austen would also start writing about other orphaned characters like Jane Fairfax and Harriet Smith in *Emma*. Throughout her novels, the orphan's story is about the freedom of self-invention. An orphan is free of something Jane Austen wrote about often with her other characters: the powers of familial persuasion. While characters like Elizabeth Bennet are constantly fighting against the expectations and influence of their parents, orphans like Fanny Price are free from the constraints of family and open to the wide world beyond home.

THE MORE YOU KNOW

Austen family remembrances point to some romantic drama unfolding with two of Jane Austen's nieces. In addition to the romantic entanglements that will be embarked upon by Godmersham niece Fanny Knight (more on that later!), James Austen's daughter Anna will cause her own romantic drama with a sudden, unsanctioned engagement. Originally living at Steventon, Anna was sent away, according to family lore, to stay with her Uncle Edward at Godmersham, and then was sent away again when she started a flirtation with Ben Lefroy, the cousin of the Tom Lefroy Jane had flirted with. Anna would eventually marry Ben Lefroy.

Jane On Top

By the autumn of 1813 Jane Austen had not only published her first novels to reach print, *Sense and Sensibility* (under the byline "By a Lady") and *Pride and Prejudice* (under the byline "By the author of 'Sense and Sensibility'"), but the first edition of both novels had sold, and a second edition of each was on the way. After her stay at Godmersham, Jane joined Henry in London and the new manuscript of *Mansfield Park* was negotiated with Thomas Egerton on commission that November. And word was getting around: England's aristocracy and royal family were talking about her books! The Duchess of Devonshire's sister, Harriet, wrote to her lover Lord Granville Leveson-Gower about this "clever novel" that "ends stupidly." As it happens, Harriet's other high-profile lover, playwright Richard Sheridan, was also reading and recommending Austen's novels. *Pride and Prejudice* had also sold well by this point, earning Austen her first independent income.

Officially, the close family was keeping Jane's authorship a secret, but word was getting out, largely, Austen herself thought, because Henry couldn't help bragging in London. And as her books started to get notice, Austen wrote to her brother Frank about the "Mystery" of her authorship. She was "trying to harden" herself to the idea of becoming known but said that she'd rather the books make "all the Money than all the Mystery." Jane was starting to take a more prominent role in her family, her circle, and her own life.

In March 1814, less than two months before *Mansfield Park* was released, Jane wrote to her sister about Henry's reactions to the novel. It's a rare insight into Jane's watchful stance as an author as her works first encountered her readers. "Henry has this moment said that he likes my M.P. better & better," she wrote in her letter to Cassandra. Her brother first "admires" the character of Henry Crawford, then puzzles over "whether H. C. would be reformed, or would forget Fanny in a fortnight," and finally declares the novel as he finishes it "extremely interesting." Despite the praise from her brother, Jane Austen's third published novel was never officially reviewed at the time. However, it sold steadily, bringing a profit of about £350. It was originally intended to be published in April, but was released on May 9.

The More You Know

The public didn't officially learn that Jane Austen was the author of her novels until it was announced in Henry's biographical introduction to the posthumously published *Northanger Abbey* and *Persuasion* in 1817.

Friendships and Writing Emma

As Jane Austen's work was emerging in the world, she seemed to have become less interested in social events, joking in an 1813 letter that the job of chaperone suited her. The pleasures of a ball were now an opportunity to be "put on the Sofa near the fire & can drink as much wine as I like." Her circle was shrinking to include her siblings; her lifelong friends the Bigg sisters Alethea and Catherine; her close friend and housemate Martha Lloyd; and her many nephews and nieces.

Her own social circle narrowed, Jane Austen started writing a new novel about community, care, and friendship. Likely written between January 1814 and March 1815, *Emma* would be her fourth published novel. Its story follows Emma Woodhouse as she realizes that she hasn't been a good friend. This is primarily seen in the "friendship" between Emma and Jane Fairfax, who lives with her aunt Miss Bates and her grandmother Mrs. Bates. Jane Fairfax, who is accomplished and reserved, contends with financial hardship and limited resources—all in contrast to the privilege and carelessness Austen assigns to her heroine, Emma. Emma can't "forgive" Jane Fairfax for her reserve surrounding her encounters in

Weymouth with Frank Churchill. She has always resented Jane's accomplishments. Ultimately, Emma openly flirts with Frank in a way that is painful for Jane.

An entire chapter of the novel follows Emma's attempts to repair the friendship once she's realized the error of her ways. She visits Jane but is told Jane is too sick to see her; she sends a note inviting Jane to Hartfield, but it is "refused, and by a verbal message." Emma then hears of the apothecary Mr. Perry's unease about Jane, whose "spirits seemed overcome." This appears to be a Regency-style nervous breakdown, and Emma writes another note, then calls on Jane in person, but Jane again refuses to see her. Hurt by her circumstances and the treatment of those around her, Jane is suffering, and also realizing she's not obligated to see Emma or anyone else.

Literary Connections

Harriet Smith, meanwhile, is also going to break away from the control that her friendship with Emma has placed on her, to find her own path to a certain charming farmer, whether Emma approves or not.

A Taste of High Society

When Jane started writing *Emma* in January 1814, she may have drawn inspiration from the Austen family adventures a few years before, when Edward first took his family to explore their own estate of Chawton in 1807. According to Austen biographer Deirdre Le Faye and Fanny Knight's diaries, the Austen women joined Edward's family at the estate for a ten-day house party. The Austen and Knight families also enjoyed an afternoon among romantic ruins, when Henry supposedly "rushed down from London" for a picnic at Netley Abbey.

This Austen family scene could have inspired the scene Austen depicts in *Emma* in 1814—a scene that acts as a turning point for the main character. Along with a mismatched group of friends and family, Emma Woodhouse is picnicking on the picturesque Box Hill. All is set for a lovely day, but the tone suggests a storm is brewing beneath the picnic's civilized rituals: There is a "languor, a want of spirits, a want of unison, which could not be got over." People aren't mixing. For Emma, the situation is "downright dullness," and even typically charming Frank Churchill is "silent and stupid."

Partly out of boredom, Emma and Frank start doing a thing the narrator says has "no English word but flirtation." Not only are Emma and Frank flirting in the presence of Jane Fairfax, his secret fiancée, but also while Mr. Knightley, Emma's close friend and hinted love interest, is watching. Emma is then outright rude to her elder family friend, Miss Bates, further shocking Knightley. Knowing she is wrong, she can only turn away when he scolds, "badly done, indeed!"

It's on this picnic at Box Hill that *Emma* reaches a point where community, friendship, and affection come together and then fall apart, largely because of the boredom and thoughtlessness of one privileged young person wreaking havoc—but on the verge of a swerve. She's about to turn a page in her story—just as Jane continued to turn the pages in her own.

LITERARY CONNECTIONS

After Mr. Knightley scolds Emma Woodhouse at the Box Hill picnic, her character is headed for what romance historian Pamela Regis calls "ritual death": the near disaster that threatens to blow up a story. Emma has to face the possibility that she's lost the esteem and friendship of her neighbors, and of Knightley, forever.

Who Gets to Go to Weymouth

The main characters in Jane Austen's novels are often faced with frustrating situations, including the titular character of *Emma.* Emma Woodhouse has never seen the sea, not to mention the seaside town of Weymouth, England, but despite asking about it, Jane Fairfax won't give her any details about Weymouth—or the man she encountered there.

Jane Austen also voiced her own frustrations to her sister, Cassandra. Although they had a more stable living situation by this time, Jane and Cassandra were still dependent on their brothers to get from one place to the next. And making plans at a time when people had to communicate through letters sent by coach meant there was a lot of uncertainty and waiting. Waiting that Jane and her sister often referred to in their letters. They would discuss how their status as single, unemployed women made them an inconvenience to those around them, and the difficulties of working around their brothers' plans in order to make their own. A year earlier, in September 1813, while in London Jane had described being at the theater with Henry, in a private box, discussing logistics. Cassandra was relying on him for travel, and was trying to fit in with his "shooting," socializing, and journeys between London, Chawton, and

Godmersham. When the conversation failed to resolve into a plan, Jane wrote, "I could not but catch at it for you."

A younger Jane had turned the frustration into a joke, writing to Cassandra in 1796: "This morning has been spent in Doubt & Deliberation; in forming plans and removing Difficulties." Her brother Frank had needed to leave the home they were visiting—their brother Edward's country house in Rowling—and the brothers wanted Jane to accompany Frank in order to get her partly home, but now, she wrote, she had been talked out of traveling with Frank lest she get stranded in a strange town where, Jane joked, "I should inevitably fall a Sacrifice to the arts of some fat Woman who would make me drunk with Small Beer—" At the end of this letter of logistics, Jane wrote, "How ill I have written! I begin to hate myself."

Like twenty-one-year-old Emma Woodhouse, Jane Austen sometimes felt inconvenient, stranded, and exasperated as she navigated being a single woman in the Georgian era.

THE MORE YOU KNOW

Mail coaches were introduced in the 1780s, making connecting with her friends and family a bit faster and easier for Jane than the years prior, when mail was delivered on horseback. Mail coaches were more effective than the earlier system of delivering on horseback because coaches didn't require switching riders or taking as many stops, and mail wasn't as frequently lost or stolen.

A Powerful Woman

While *Mansfield Park*'s Fanny Price is thought to be goodness personified, *Emma*'s Emma Woodhouse embodies capriciousness. Jane Austen was contemplating the novel she'd just finished, and perhaps also contemplating this new novel she would start in just a few months while enjoying the luxuries of Godmersham, its grand library with its fireplace and walls of books, its lavish meals—and its family mayhem—but there are few similarities between the two books.

With the character of Emma Woodhouse, Austen shows readers how power can sometimes be a bad thing, depending on how it's used. This heroine has wealth, good looks, "and very little to distress or vex her." She lives at home caring for her high-maintenance father, Mr. Woodhouse, which is confining at times, but also grants Emma a lot of affection, regard, and security. And she uses her copious leisure time and all the powers at her disposal to dominate a younger, seventeen-year-old friend, Harriet Smith. This influence won't go down well with Emma's friend, Mr. Knightly, and she will have a lot to learn about using her powers for good. . . .

Austen used *Emma* to show Regency readers that unlike the passive females portrayed by her era's conduct books, women characters could be *worse* than some might imagine—just as easily as they could be better. Women in the Regency, whether at Godmersham or Emma's Hartfield, didn't easily fit into conduct books. And some didn't wield their privilege and power in the best ways.

LITERARY CONNECTIONS

The power of women was a hot-button issue in the world Austen was growing up in and writing about. Others were also using the page to express their views. In Mary Robinson's 1799 *Letter to the Women of England on the Injustice of Mental Subordination*, the former actress and mistress of the Prince Regent urged an end to sexual double standards and advocated for equality, asking, "this plain and rational question,—is not woman a human being, gifted with all the feelings that inhabit the bosom of man?"

A Real-Life Emma

On one Saturday in November 1813, Jane Austen wrote from Godmersham about a party at Chilham Castle. She had been "well entertained by bits & scraps" at the party, writing about the wife of Dr. Britton, who "amuses me very much with her affected refinement & elegance." The real-life characters Austen describes in her letters from this autumn at Godmersham reflect the characters that would emerge in the next year to inhabit the Highbury world of *Emma*. Perhaps like Dr. Britton's "affected" wife, Emma's Mrs. Augusta Elton can't be in a grand place without comparing it to the grand house of her sister, Mrs. Selina Suckling. And Miss Milles, a woman Jane had visited just a few days before the party, mirrors the fictional Miss Bates. As Austen wrote to Cassandra in October, Miss Milles "provided us with plenty to laugh at . . . using such odd expressions & so foolishly minute that I could hardly keep my countenance."

But perhaps most notable is how Jane Austen's own niece, Fanny, compares to the heroine of *Emma*. Like Emma's, Fanny's mother had passed away when Fanny was young, and she was raised on her father's grand estates. When Fanny was about fourteen years old, she first visited Edward Austen's grand estate at Chawton House. Fanny explored the stately sixteenth-century passageways, halls, and galleries (one supposedly haunted!), writing to a friend that it was all too easy to get lost in the house "& I don't know when I shall be quite mistress of all the intricate, & different ways." Like Austen's niece Fanny Austen Knight, Emma Woodhouse is motherless, at leisure in a grand house, and "accountable to no one but her father."

As Jane described Fanny in a letter to her, Fanny was "the oddest Creature! —Nervous enough in some respects, but in others perfectly without nerves!" According to her correspondence with her aunt, Fanny had the run of a grand house, whether at Chawton or Godmersham, and presumably could indulge her whims—just like Emma Woodhouse at the Highbury estate. Characters in *Emma* experience all the confusions of flirting, conducting secret affairs, and falling in love, with the main character taking advantage of her status to injure feelings and manipulate relationships. But Emma will also evolve over the course of the novel, and Austen's letters are full of hope that her niece would grow and thrive too.

The More You Know

Actresses Gwyneth Paltrow and Anya Taylor-Joy took on the role of Emma in period adaptations of the novel. Paltrow's *Emma* was released in 1996 and Taylor-Joy's *Emma* was released in 2020. Both films were a success and led to a resurging interest in Austen's works.

From Emma, Chapter 26

They sang together once more; and Emma would then resign her place to Miss Fairfax, whose performance, both vocal and instrumental, she never could attempt to conceal from herself, was infinitely superior to her own.

With mixed feelings, she seated herself at a little distance from the numbers round the instrument, to listen. Frank Churchill sang again. They had sung together once or twice, it appeared, at Weymouth. But the sight of Mr. Knightley among the most attentive, soon drew away half Emma's mind . . .

Arguing in Austen

The idea of how two romantic partners might improve each other—or not—is examined throughout Jane Austen's novels and also her personal letters. In one situation in Austen's own life in 1813, she and her friend Harriot Moore were picked up from Canterbury half an hour late by a coachman, and Harriot's husband got angry. Jane, who had been continuously observing the husband, wrote to Cassandra, "I wanted to see him angry" and noted that she was relieved "he did not scold Harriot at all."

This insight into Austen's life, along with the many arguments played out in her novels, reveals her thoughts on the way that a person conducts themselves in a disagreement has meaning—and consequences. To Austen, an argument can either help those involved improve or make everything worse. Particularly, the arguments Austen was writing between Emma Woodhouse and Mr. Knightley at this time show readers two people who have met their match. Emma debates effectively even while she is obviously wrong, driving Mr. Knightley to distraction. But Knightley's own arguments show what a genuine friend he can be despite his anger; he is concerned about Emma and the ways people like Frank Churchill may be influencing her. And he eventually forgives her. Through *Emma*, Austen gives readers a heroine who learns to channel her strengths away from their misuse, and into the betterment of her community, by arguing with (and ultimately listening to) a friend.

The More You Know

In a letter to her sister, Cassandra, Jane Austen once wrote, "Marriage is a great Improver." In her letter, she was sharing the news that a family friend named Edward Bridges—who Austen's family speculated may have proposed to Jane herself—was getting married. Jane called this information "quite news" and said, "I wish him happy with all my heart. . . . As to Money, that will come You may be sure, because they cannot do without it.—When you see him again, pray give him our Congratulations and best wishes."

From Emma, Chapter 8

"Oh! to be sure," cried Emma, "it is always incomprehensible to a man that a woman should ever refuse an offer of marriage. A man always imagines a woman to be ready for any body who asks her."

"Nonsense! a man does not imagine any such thing. But what is the meaning of this? Harriet Smith refuse Robert Martin? madness, if it is so; but I hope you are mistaken."

"I saw her answer!—nothing could be clearer."

"You saw her answer!—you wrote her answer too. Emma, this is your doing. You persuaded her to refuse him."

"And if I did, (which, however, I am far from allowing) I should not feel that I had done wrong."

The Regency Working Class

Throughout Jane Austen's life, an entire group of people did the churning, lifting, mending, driving, cooking, and work that powered the grand houses of Georgian England like the ones Austen visited. This group were the real-life workers who made their way into Austen's writing. Dozens of laborers are mentioned by Jane Austen in her letters, about seventy-three of them named. There's Dinah, Mary Doe, John Bond, Mrs. Driver, and Mrs. Hall. There's the unnamed worker who tried to save Austen's friend Anne Brydges Lefroy when her horse bolted, causing a fatal accident. There's Nanny Hillard. There's Molly, who encouraged Jane to enjoy herself in the sea at Bath, and Jenny and James, who Jane was glad to see "are walked to Charmouth" to get books and a newspaper for James, a reader.

While members of the working class aren't showcased often in her novels, a few hardworking characters do make an impression in them—particularly in *Emma*. In *Emma*, Austen introduces the tenant farmer Robert Martin as someone Harriet Smith has a crush on. While Emma says he isn't worth paying attention to, he ends up being a key part of the book's happily-ever-after, as well as an example of how friendship goes beyond social status.

Despite being classes apart, Mr. Knightley describes Martin as "one of his best friends." According to Knightley, Martin is someone for whom he has "a thorough regard . . . open, straightforward, and very well-judging." And in a straightforward happily-ever-after, Robert Martin does eventually get the girl! He and the object of his love from the beginning of the story, Harriet Smith, marry toward the end of the book.

LITERARY CONNECTIONS

In her 2013 novel *Longbourn*, author Jo Baker elevates the workers of the Bennet household of *Pride and Prejudice* to main characters. Elizabeth and her four sisters are seen through the eyes of the people who dress them, organize them, and care for them. Baker says she was inspired by her own family history and her own British grandmother and great-aunts who worked in domestic service. She was also motivated by one passage from *Pride and Prejudice* revealing that there was "such a succession of rain" on the day of the much-anticipated Netherfield ball that "The very shoe-roses for Netherfield were got by proxy." The line caused Baker to question: Whose job was it to go out in "such a succession of rain" to get the luxury item of shoe-roses, when no one else was going out? Her exploration of that question led to one of the most critically-acclaimed Austen retellings.

Love and Class

The grand estates, gardens, farms, and castles of Austen's novels like *Emma* are about much more than a place to live: They supply the land and wealth that grant a person power in the nineteenth century. And in—as Lady Catherine says—"the shades" of grand places like Pemberley and Donwell Abbey are the characters who not only power the engine that keeps the whole enterprise going, but also manage their own homes, lives, aspirations, and relationships.

Mr. Robert Martin, the gentleman farmer in *Emma*, isn't just a friend of Knightley and the eventual husband of Harriet Smith. Emma at first points out Robert Martin's "entire want of gentility" and declares him "so very clownish, so totally without air. I had imagined him, I confess, a degree or two nearer gentility." But in key ways, the portrayal of the Martin family has parallels to the Austen family. Robert Martin reads poetry aloud with his family—just like the Austens. Not only that, but he reads from *Elegant Extracts*, a collection of passages from sermons, histories, and literature the Austen family also read. Like Jane Austen, Martin is interested in self-improvement and study as well as practical pursuits, and enjoys reading fiction like *The Vicar of Wakefield*, a popular romance novel of the day. And like the Austens, he farms and raises livestock to earn a living. Austen describes his home, Abbey-Mill Farm, as two comfortable parlors, one summer-house with room to entertain twelve, one "upper maid" who's been with the family twenty-five years, and eight cows.

In this idyllic view of a farmer and his family who read together, care for and find joy in each other, and tend their household—down to Mrs. Martin's favorite Welch cow—Jane Austen offers a view not unlike her own family.

THE MORE YOU KNOW

The Chawton archive at Jane Austen's House has a copy of *Elegant Extracts* that was owned by Austen and given to her niece Anna. It was later passed along to Anna's daughter Jemima. In this copy, there are markings (possibly three generations' worth!) alongside passages on piety and literary style. Three inscriptions in the front show Anna's name, Jemima's name, and "the gift of her aunt Jane."

Eighteenth-Century Games

Games were a big part of Jane Austen's world. Speculation, whist, vingt-un, and quadrille were all played by the Austen family and get mentions in her letters. Austen herself loved playing games like cards, riddles and conundrums, and paper ships with her nephews, but she often declined to play games like commerce—a Georgian game similar to poker—where money was at stake.

As Austen knew, games can also reveal details about the people who play them. Game theory is the study of not only a game play but also the calculation and motivation of the player; it's one lens that Austen fans and scholars can look through to uncover more about her characters and overarching themes. Through the games in her novels, readers get to watch Austen's characters bet, gamble, play—and get played. In *Mansfield Park,* a game of speculation reveals the inner traits of key characters. Henry Crawford is able to carry on a conversation while playing both his own hand and Lady Bertram's; Fanny Price sacrifices her own hand to help William; and Mary Crawford remarks that if she loses, it will not be from lack of trying. Then there is *Emma,* where the plot turns on a game of "anagrams" (one player gives another a word that they then have to scramble into something else).

Frank gives Jane words—including the word "blunder"—that refer to a secret between them. This makes Jane uncomfortable enough to leave the table, clues Knightley into the secret and Frank's mistreatment of Jane, and also reveals how Emma—missing the whole thing—remains carelessly ignorant to what's happening in the lives of those around her.

But Highbury might be the place where game theory is most helpful. When Emma is anticipating Mr. Philip Elton's proposal to Harriet Smith, it's not just one but two Knightleys—Mr. George Knightley and his brother, John—who warn Emma that Mr. Elton is not going to propose to Harriet. John makes it clear that Elton is interested in Emma herself. To which Emma—smug but miscalculating—laughs, musing about how someone of such intelligence can be so wrong. It's only in giving up the game that Emma will stand a chance at winning!

THE MORE YOU KNOW

The publisher John Murray offered to buy the copyright for *Emma* for £450 along with the copyrights for *Mansfield Park*, which had sold out its first printing in 1814, and *Sense and Sensibility*. Wanting to retain the copyright, Austen refused the offer and instead arranged to publish *Emma* with Murray on commission. In an October 1815 letter Austen wrote to Cassandra of the publisher, "he is a Rogue of course, but a civil one." *Emma* was published December 23, 1815.

From Emma, Chapter 49

"I stopped you ungraciously, just now, Mr. Knightley, and, I am afraid, gave you pain.—But if you have any wish to speak openly to me as a friend, or to ask my opinion of any thing that you may have in contemplation—as a friend, indeed, you may command me.—I will hear whatever you like. I will tell you exactly what I think."

"As a friend!"—repeated Mr. Knightley.—"Emma, that I fear is a word—No, I have no wish—Stay, yes, why should I hesitate?—I have gone too far already for concealment.—Emma, I accept your offer—Extraordinary as it may seem, I accept it, and refer myself to you as a friend.—Tell me, then, have I no chance of ever succeeding?"

He stopped in his earnestness to look the question, and the expression of his eyes overpowered her.

Friends to Lovers

Friends to lovers is a trope of romantic fiction, where characters begin as good friends and eventually fall in love. Whether in Hampshire or Highbury, the friends-to-lovers plot celebrates the idea of a slow-growing love among two people who know each other better than anyone. It's one of the most popular tropes of the contemporary romance novel, combining themes that are fun, enticing, and familiar all at once. Jane Austen can be seen as an early inspiration for this trope, which wasn't recognized during her time. She had even seen a real example of the then-unknown friends-to-lovers trope happen close to home: Her oldest brother, James, married family friend Mary Lloyd, the sister of Jane's very best friend, Martha Lloyd, in 1797.

During a visit to Godmersham in 1808, Jane Austen wrote in a letter that "it is pleasant to be among people who know one's connection and care about them." Now Austen was weaving this trope through *Emma*, creating the romance between heroine Emma Woodhouse and her friend Mr. Knightley. At the start of the story, Emma's sister is married to Knightley's brother, and Emma and Knightley have grown up together. A mutual understanding and their shared histories, futures, and interests—also the way they exasperate each other—all signal to readers that these two are meant for each other. Friends to lovers is a popular and often comforting trope in romance stories where the lovers find stability together. In *Emma,* Knightley and Emma have the security of two estates and a family that has already been intertwined for years.

THE MORE YOU KNOW

In Amy Heckerling's 1995 film *Clueless,* which is loosely based on *Emma,* the lead characters Josh (Knightley) and Cher (Emma), are step-siblings growing up in the Los Angeles suburbs. It's when the shiftless Cher hits a mini-crisis that she realizes that a guy who's vetted by and loyal to her own beloved father has its upsides. Like Emma and Knightley, it's not only the friends-to-lovers trope but also a matter of *family-friends-becoming-lovers*, with all of the security that a lifelong family connection brings.

Austen Family Matchmakers

Similar to her character Emma Woodhouse, Jane Austen had a lifelong habit of matchmaking! Throughout her life and letters, she joked about finding husbands for various "Misses," and gave advice to her nieces and nephews—sometimes jokingly, sometimes very seriously—about their love lives. On one occasion she mixed this matchmaking with the pastime of party games, when she wrote to Cassandra describing a party in Southampton that involved a quadrille table and a game of commerce, declaring: "I have got a Husband for each of the Miss Maitlands" before moving on to other neighborhood gossip.

And Jane got the matchmaking treatment right back from her own family: There was even a family conspiracy to set her up with a Chawton neighbor, Mr. Papillon, as early as 1808. She occasionally joined in on the joke, updating family members on the progress of her "courtship" with Mr. Papillon. In a letter to her nephew James Edward Austen-Leigh, she joked, "I am happy to tell you that Mr. Papillon will soon make his offer, probably next Monday, as he returns on Saturday.—His intentions can be no longer doubtful in the smallest degree." The supportive family friend Mrs. Knight was also interested in Jane's love life, as Jane wrote to

Cassandra, "I am very much obliged to Mrs. Knight for such a proof of the interest she takes in me—& she may depend upon it, that I will marry Mr. Papillon, whatever may be his reluctance or my own—I owe her much more than such a trifling sacrifice."

Austen's updates on romance showcase the humor fans know and love from her novels. They also show the playful and loving family banter she would engage in up until her final days.

The More You Know

The collection of Jane Austen's letters compiled and indexed by Deirdre Le Faye contains more than one hundred matches—real and imagined—for the people in Austen's life, from family and neighbors to royalty and domestic workers. "I have a Southampton Match to return for your Kentish one," she joked with her sister, Cassandra, in a November 1808 letter.

Marriage Choices

Jane Austen's matchmaking wasn't kept just to some mysterious "Misses." With three novels about love and marriage now published and *Emma* in the works, Jane was also acting as a matchmaker and mentor to her niece Fanny Knight as Fanny entered the world of romance. At around this time, Fanny, the eldest daughter of the large Godmersham estate, was at an age when she started attracting suitors. She poured out her heart in secret letters to her aunt Jane, who advised her to stay alert and to use her head as well as her heart in decisions of love. In 1814, Austen wrote to her niece that she thought her very capable "of being really in love." She warned the then twenty-one-year-old Fanny about "how full of temptation the next 6 or 7 years of your life will probably be—(it is the very period of Life for the <u>strongest</u> attachments to be formed)." In a letter to Fanny that very same year she also claimed, "Anything is to be preferred or endured rather than marrying without Affection."

But marrying with or without affection wasn't a prevailing choice at the time. Courtship and marriage rituals were often motivated by improvement of social standing, and typically, the local church (with the reading of "the banns," an ancient legal tradition announcing the pending marriage), the couple's families, and the community were involved in the marriage process. Austen had already alluded to this through many of her characters, from Charlotte Lucas and Lady Catherine in *Pride and Prejudice*, to Mr. Elton in *Emma*. These characters all see marriage as a means of gaining property, wealth, or other forms of security.

While Jane Austen understood the need to find security, she also gives credit to the philosophy of marrying for love. Throughout her novels, the heroines and heroes—from Henry Tilney and Catherine Morland to Edward Ferrars and Elinor Dashwood—choose true love. Crucially though, these characters are also practical about their love and what is needed for a marriage to last: Henry and Catherine gain the approval of General Tilney, and Elinor and Edward gain the approval of Mrs. Ferrars.

LITERARY CONNECTIONS

Elizabeth Bennet's best friend, Charlotte Lucas, dismays the heroine with her pragmatic decision to marry Mr. Collins. Elizabeth has trouble empathizing with her friend, but contemporary audiences are more understanding. Charlotte Lucas has turned into a social-media symbol for the importance of stability, home, and comfort in an uncertain world. Her quote from the 2005 *Pride & Prejudice* film adaptation, "I'm twenty-seven years old. I've no money and no prospects. I'm already a burden to my parents and I'm frightened," has even been piped onto birthday cakes!

A "One in a Thousand" Man

In Jane Austen's correspondence with her niece, Fanny Knight, about challenges in love, Austen discussed what she felt made an ideal partner. She noted not only the specific qualities she thought were important in this kind of partner, but also things like time and circumstance that couldn't be controlled but were also crucial to finding that happily-ever-after. The person they both thought "perfection" might be "one in a Thousand," Austen said in a November 1814 letter, a character "where Grace & Spirit are united to Worth, where the Manners are equal to the Heart & Understanding." But such a one, Jane wrote, "may not come in your way . . . "

Choosing the *right* partner is even more complicated in Austen's novels because of the *wrong* choices that are also out there. Enter a parade of Mr. Wrongs, including Mr. John Willoughby from *Sense and Sensibility*, Mr. George Wickham from *Pride and Prejudice*, Mr. Henry Crawford from *Mansfield Park*, and now Mr. Frank Churchill from *Emma*. Willoughby arrives as a rescuer on horseback, Wickham arrives in splendid colors as an officer of the militia, and Crawford and Churchill arrive with their games and their charm. Enlightenment philosopher Adam Smith helps make sense of this retinue of Mr. Wrongs: In contrast to "the proud man" like a Mr. Darcy, the "vain man," Smith writes, "wishes you to view him in much more splendid colors than those in which . . . he can really view himself." In other words, a man like Wickham or Willoughby would like you to admire him even as he knows he is lacking in admirable qualities. The shoe fits! Jane Austen creates every one of her antiheroes to be Smithian fakers and flatterers.

Meanwhile, Austen heroes like proud Mr. Darcy and exacting Mr. Knightley are honest men who may need to be taken down a notch or two by a heroine but ultimately have what Adam Smith described—sincerity, truth, and integrity—to back up their self-possession. Whether when writing to her niece or channeling Smith's philosophies in her novels, Austen was often analyzing the qualities of heroes and heroines.

LITERARY CONNECTIONS

Jane Austen may have been warning readers about Wickham from the first mention of his name: Some scholars suggest that his name is a clever combination of "wicked" and "hamlet" (home), making him "a wicked man in society."

"A Man & an Angel"

Jane Austen was more serious about matchmaking when it came to her niece, Fanny, than in *Emma* or her own misadventures in romance. The daughter of Jane's brother Edward, Fanny was only seventeen years younger than Austen, "almost another Sister," she wrote, and the two were often together during family holidays and Jane's long visits at Edward's estates. They also enjoyed lengthy visits with Jane's brother Henry in London that included trips to the theater, shopping, and socializing. And during one London stay in the fall of 1815, a real-life flirtation unfolded right in front of Jane, between her niece and a "Mr. Haden."

Charles Thomas Haden—an apothecary and frequent visitor to Henry's house—was intelligent, conversational, musical, and medical, with a degree from Edinburgh. During that visit in November 1815, Jane wrote to her sister Cassandra about "Fanny & Mr. Haden in two chairs (I beleive [sic] at least they had two chairs) talking together uninterruptedly.—Fancy the scene!" Cassandra appears to have questioned the suitability of an apothecary as a match for Fanny. But Jane responded, "You call him an Apothecary; he is no Apothecary, he has never been an Apothecary, there is not an Apothecary in this Neighbourhood . . . he is a Haden, nothing but a Haden, a sort of wonderful nondescript Creature on two Legs, something between a Man & an Angel—but without the least spice of an Apothecary.—He is perhaps the only Person not an Apothecary hereabouts." Through absurdity, Jane challenged the categories that society placed people in, and the assumptions her peers had about what made someone a worthy suitor.

THE MORE YOU KNOW

Despite Jane Austen's seeming approval of Mr. Haden, Fanny Knight would ultimately marry a titled suitor, becoming the second wife of Sir Edward Knatchbull in 1820. As Lady Knatchbull, she would go on to have nine children. Her eldest son, Lord Brabourne, later found these letters between Jane, Cassandra, and his mother, and shared them with the world (more on this later!).

Writing Persuasion

By the spring of 1815, Jane Austen had finished writing *Emma*, and was now working on a new novel. Forty years old, she sat down to write what would be her final published novel: *Persuasion.* Often considered a meditation on time, *Persuasion* had a more somber tone than her previous novels, and introduced a deep-thinking and soulful heroine to literary history.

Anne Elliot is about twenty-seven years old and her "bloom" has "vanished early." Nearly eight years earlier, she had rejected a romance with a young navy officer after some persuading from a well-meaning mentor. The navy officer had little money and an unpredictable future, and Anne was convinced by a trusted family friend and advisor that the marriage wouldn't be a secure one. Unfortunately, she also feels this lost romance was her best and only chance at happiness in love.

Persuasion is a novel that follows the effects of a years-long separation between two people meant to be together who are then forced back into each other's lives. As Austen herself said, "But seven years I suppose are enough to change every pore of one's skin, & every feeling of one's mind." It was a thought she had expressed in a letter back in April

1805, just a few months after her father's death. She was twenty-nine years old at the time, just two years older than her heroine Anne Elliot. Nearing forty, she now knew just how much could change over time.

Fortunately for Anne, *Persuasion* is all about second chances, and after eight years of regret, she will have her happily-ever-after.

The More You Know

Actress Dakota Johnson portrayed Anne Elliot in a 2022 movie adaptation of *Persuasion*. An attempt at a more modernized retelling of the novel that doesn't follow the chronology of Austen's story, the film wasn't well received by fans or critics.

From Persuasion, Chapter 4

A few months had seen the beginning and the end of their acquaintance; but not with a few months ended Anne's share of suffering from it. Her attachment and regrets had, for a long time, clouded every enjoyment of youth, and an early loss of bloom and spirits had been their lasting effect.

More than seven years were gone since this little history of sorrowful interest had reached its close; and time had softened down much, perhaps nearly all of peculiar attachment to him, but she had been too dependent on time alone . . .

Captain Wentworth and the Napoleonic Wars

"What weather! & what news!" Jane had written in her last letter from Godmersham on November 6–7, 1813. The news was that French general Napoleon Bonaparte, who had been battling the British naval forces and rampaging across Europe throughout most of Austen's life so far, had been defeated in a campaign. Ten years after the wars had started in May of 1803, the tides were beginning to turn.

After his exile to the island of Elba in 1814 and subsequent escape to resume fighting for one hundred days, Napoleon was finally defeated again in the 1815 Battle of Waterloo. Jane Austen sat down to write *Persuasion* on the exact day, August 8, 1815, that the newspapers announced Napoleon's final exile. It came after decades of uncertainty and war—as the writer Collins Hemingway notes, twenty-nine years out of Jane Austen's total of forty-one.

The Napoleonic Wars were an impactful part of Austen's world, and also served as the backdrop for one of her most captivating literary heroes: *Persuasion*'s Captain Frederick Wentworth of the Royal Navy. As scholar Jocelyn Harris explains in her book *A Revolution Almost Beyond Expression*, Wentworth has, without sponsorship or a network of contacts, overcome the odds to capture powerful French frigates. Meanwhile, heroine Anne Elliot follows his progress in the Navy List, which reports the capture and activity of naval ships and their captains in the newspapers. Once he's home, Anne listens as Wentworth talks of battles and exploits like subduing privateers, winning a fortune in prize money, and cruises of distant seas. Borrowing, Harris suggests, from British heroes like Lord Nelson and Captain Scott, and from Lord Byron's characters from the *Turkish Tales* with their "bright, proud eye," Austen portrays a hero for the ages.

The only drawback from *Persuasion*'s happy ending is a watchful one, as the narrator warns that Anne "gloried in being a sailor's wife," but she "must pay the tax of quick alarm" and possible danger.

Literary Connections

In her essay "The 'Unfeudal Tone of the Present Day,'" Austen scholar Claudia Johnson examines the competing systems of values in *Persuasion* between the haughty aristocracy and Sir Walter's book of "Baronetage," and the meritocratic achievements of Captain Wentworth and the Navy List. With his fortune and "mythic"-level accomplishments, Johnson writes, Wentworth is not only meritocratic but is "nouveau riche" (newly wealthy) "with a vengeance."

Navy Wives

Jane Austen herself understood the perspective of a watchful Anne Elliot studying newspapers for accounts of the activity abroad and vigilantly nurturing hopes of peace. Austen's older brother Frank and younger brother Charles were both part of the Royal Navy during the Napoleonic Wars. "I give you all Joy of Frank's return, which happens in the true Sailor way," Austen wrote to Cassandra from Godmersham back in 1808, "just after our being told not to expect him for some weeks.—The wind has been very much against him, but I suppose he must be in our Neighbourhood by this time. Fanny is in hourly expectation of him here." This everyday account to Cassandra evokes so much of what Austen observes and contemplates through her characters. The return of Fanny Price's sailor brother William to Mansfield Park brings such joy and belonging; while Anne Elliot's beloved Frederick Wentworth is first cast out and then returns to the neighborhood unexpectedly, now wealthy, accomplished, and a victorious captain.

These themes of the passing of time and fate will continually be linked to navy life throughout *Persuasion*, as they were in Jane's own life. Both Frank and Charles Austen chose meritocratic professions in the navy that would require them to rest their fortunes on chance—from the literal forces of the wind at sea, to the potential for disease and danger of the sort that had already taken Cassandra Austen's fiancé, Tom Fowle. The youngest, Charles, is the one whose life seems most intertwined with both the fortunes and the misfortunes of navy life: He met his wife, the Bermuda-born Fanny Palmer, at sea and Fanny gave birth to and raised their children on board ships with Charles. Eventually, Fanny would die following childbirth at sea, and their youngest child would pass away soon after. Charles would go on to marry Fanny's sister, Harriet, as the ideal mother for his children, and they would have four more children together.

These experiences provided a front-row seat to the Royal Navy life for Jane Austen as she created *Persuasion*'s setting and the fates that separated and reunited Anne Elliot and her hero.

LITERARY CONNECTIONS

Like the cross gifted to Fanny Price by her Royal Navy brother, William, in *Mansfield Park,* Jane and Cassandra Austen were given topaz crosses by their Navy-officer brother Charles Austen. You can find them on display at the Jane Austen's House museum in Chawton, or on the museum's website: https://janeaustens.house/.

Sophy Croft Takes the Reins

Whether *Persuasion*'s hero draws from Frank or Charles Austen or both, Captain Wentworth is described as adventurous, daring, and occasionally arrogant. And like Frank and Charles Austen, he also has a sister: Sophia Croft, who is happily married to Admiral Croft of the British Navy. Sophia—called Sophy by her husband—is a minor character whose portrayal in the novel is significant: Even though she's married to an admiral (the epitome of power and ability during the Regency era), *she* is the one who manages the couple's business affairs, and on one occasion literally takes the reins from him to prevent an accident by his distracted driving of their carriage.

She also stands up to her brother, the hero Captain Wentworth, when he says he "would never willingly admit any ladies on board a ship of his." It turns out his own sister—like Austen's own sister-in-law Fanny Palmer Austen—has not only been at sea with her husband but has also spent some of what she insists are "the happiest part of my life" on a ship. In reply to her brother's comment she says, "I hate to hear you talking so, like a fine gentleman, as if women were all fine ladies, instead of rational creatures. We none of us expect to be in smooth waters all our days."

Sophy Croft—and Austen herself—entered into the then eighteenth- and nineteenth-century debates about the nature of gender and gender roles. Some of Austen's characters illustrate those debates calling for women to be seen as rational and capable, as equal to men and not needing to be protected and segregated from them. It would be many years before there was any reform for women in the real world, but Austen's strong female characters call to mind the debates unfolding in the background as she wrote *Persuasion.*

THE MORE YOU KNOW

"I could no more write a Romance than an Epic Poem," Jane Austen wrote to her pen pal the Reverend James Stanier Clarke. Yet Austen's novels revolve around courtships. She clarified in her letter: "I could not sit seriously down to write a serious Romance under any other motive than to save my Life." With that repetition—both words *seriously* and *serious* appearing in the same sentence—Austen was emphasizing that she preferred using parody to make a point.

From Persuasion, Chapter 8

" . . . I would assist any brother officer's wife that I could, and I would bring anything of Harville's from the world's end, if he wanted it. But do not imagine that I did not feel it an evil in itself."

"Depend upon it, they were all perfectly comfortable."

"I might not like them the better for that perhaps. Such a number of women and children have no *right* to be comfortable on board."

"My dear Frederick, you are talking quite idly. Pray, what would become of us poor sailors' wives, who often want to be conveyed to one port or another, after our husbands, if everybody had your feelings?"

"My feelings, you see, did not prevent my taking Mrs. Harville and all her family to Plymouth."

"But I hate to hear you talking so like a fine gentleman, and as if women were all fine ladies, instead of rational creatures. We none of us expect to be in smooth water all our days."

Good Marriages

One of the surprising aspects of Jane Austen's novels is that while they reinvented the courtship plot with its happily-ever-after, they do not portray many (or nearly any) good marriages. Even by the time she was writing her last novel, *Persuasion*, readers were still getting characters like Mary Musgrove: a young, self-absorbed wife who shirks every responsibility and over-relies on her reasonable husband, Charles. Through Mary Musgrove and other mismatched couples—from the Palmers and the Middletons of *Sense and Sensibility* to the Eltons of *Emma*—Austen reveals her thoughts on what happens when society gets what it, and its conduct books, prescribes: fragile, uneducated females.

The best example might be one of Austen's earliest: *Sense and Sensibility*'s cheery Charlotte Palmer, who has nothing to say to her husband, the grumpy Mr. Palmer. (The narrator assures readers that Mr. Palmer is not the first man to be attracted to someone only to end up with a silly wife!) In *Mansfield Park*, lackadaisical Lady Bertram can't decide even on whether to play speculation or whist, so she appeals to her husband.

Taking a page from political philosopher Mary Wollstonecraft, Austen used her writing and characters like the

Palmers and Bertrams to call for education and equality in the treatment and development of girls and women. And this message is showcased in portraits of not only bad marriages but also good ones. In her final completed novel, *Persuasion*, Austen created something fairly uncommon in her previous stories: a portrait of a solid, companionable, and happy marriage. In fact, there are two in *Persuasion*. One marriage is that of the Harvilles, the navy friends of Captain Wentworth, who have a welcoming home in Lyme. The depiction of a happy marriage then deepens with Admiral Croft and his wife, Sophia. As Austen describes, Anne, the novel's heroine, "always watched them as long as she could: delighted to fancy she understood what they might be talking of, as they walked along in happy independence . . . " The Crofts are able to tune out the status-conscious snobbery of society and of Anne Elliot's own family to focus on what matters in Austen's stories: independence, equitable companionship, and community.

The More You Know

In the 1995 movie adaptation of *Sense and Sensibility*, Imelda Staunton and Hugh Laurie play the silly Mrs. Palmer and her crotchety husband. Although Laurie's part was minor, it would help him carve a path in more serious film roles. At the time of the movie, his background was mostly comedies like *Blackadder*.

A Sad Heroine and Hints of Illness

On a summer day in 1816, Jane Austen wrote a letter full of jokes to her nephew James Edward Austen-Leigh. She described going outside that day, only to turn back to avoid "A Pelter" of rain, which was now starting up again outside her window. She had begun to feel the effects of a mysterious illness that spring. Illness aside, she was days away from finishing her last published novel, *Persuasion*.

In May 1816, Jane and Cassandra had been traveling together, and in early June they stopped in at Kintbury, the home of Cassandra's fiancé, Tom Fowle, who'd died in 1797. According to her letters, Cassandra still considered the family and the place her own. (When the Fowle family members recalled this visit later, they described Jane Austen as seeming not quite well, yet eager to revisit all the rooms of the vicarage.) Many believe it was Cassandra's experience with lost love and the memories that came up as she and Jane visited Kintbury that inspired Jane's portrait of Anne Elliot in *Persuasion*. Just like her sister, who had lost her fiancé at a young age, Anne "had been forced into prudence in her youth" when she was pressured into ending a relationship with someone she loved.

Cassandra herself appeared to have felt a connection to *Persuasion*, as her personal copy of the published book would later be found to have notes written in the margin. "Dear dear Jane! This deserves to be written in letters of gold" was written beside the description of Anne Elliot being "forced into prudence."

The More You Know

Kintbury, the family home of Cassandra Austen's fiancé, Tom Fowle, is immortalized in the BBC/PBS Masterpiece series *Miss Austen*. Released in February 2025 in the UK and May 2025 in the US, this four-part series follows Jane Austen's story, her family and friendships, and her legacy, through the perspective of her sister, Cassandra.

Finishing Persuasion

In March 1816 the Austen family had been hit by misfortune when the bank that Henry Austen owned failed and was declared bankrupt. All investments were lost, and the effects of this misfortune would ricochet through the Austen family, which was heavily invested in his bank. Jane's individual investments were small, but the bankruptcy still lowered the total income for the Austen women. The £50 annual payments they had been getting from Henry and Frank ceased.

While dealing with this financial crisis and her mysterious illness, Jane Austen finished *Persuasion*, marking the end of her manuscript *finis* (the end) on July 16. She then did some reworking and marked it *finis* again on July 18. But she still wasn't satisfied. Cassandra and James Edward later recalled that Austen felt weighed down by the ending of this novel—struggling with how to end it, and unhappy with an original draft of the ending. However, she awoke the morning of August 6 feeling refreshed and reworked the resolution once again to her satisfaction, giving the manuscript its final *finis* the same day.

With her final ending to her final novel, Austen created what critics would call one of the most beautiful love letters in literary history. Anne Elliot finally had her say, and

Wentworth answered in a letter showing that he was hearing *and* listening. The letter combined past, present, and future tenses, telling Anne, "You pierce my soul. I am half agony, half hope." Anne responded, "Such a letter was not to be soon recovered from."

LITERARY CONNECTIONS

Cassandra Austen passed along the manuscript containing the original ending of *Persuasion* to her niece, the budding writer Anna Lefroy. Author Jocelyn Harris explores this original ending and how it compares to Austen's final version in her book *A Revolution Almost Beyond Expression*.

From Persuasion, Chapter 23

. . . soon words enough had passed between them to decide their direction towards the comparatively quiet and retired gravel walk, where the power of conversation would make the present hour a blessing indeed, and prepare it for all the immortality which the happiest recollections of their own future lives could bestow. There they exchanged again those feelings and those promises which had once before seemed to secure everything, but which had been followed by so many, many years of division and estrangement. There they returned again into the past, more exquisitely happy, perhaps, in their re-union, than when it had been first projected; more tender, more tried, more fixed in a knowledge of each other's character, truth, and attachment; more equal to act, more justified in acting. And there, as they slowly paced the gradual ascent, heedless of every group around them, seeing neither sauntering politicians, bustling housekeepers, flirting girls, nor nursery-maids and children, they could indulge in those retrospections and acknowledgements, and especially in those explanations of what had directly preceded the present moment, which were so poignant and so ceaseless in interest. All the little variations of the last week were gone through; and of yesterday and to-day there could scarcely be an end.

Declining Health and Final Letters

The first known mention Jane Austen made of being ill is in a letter to Cassandra begun on September 8, 1816; this is also the last surviving letter written to her sister. At this time, Austen was at home at Chawton, and trying to figure out what was making her feel under the weather. However, she was still receiving visits from friends and family, and she mentioned that she enjoyed a "walk home by Moonlight" after dinner at the Great House. She added that her back wasn't giving her much pain and that she suspected the reason she was so unwell when Cassandra left was *because* Cassandra was leaving. She continued that she was trying to get to "as beautiful a state" as she could for a scheduled visit from "Dr. White." By the spring of 1817, the Austen family faced another setback, which Jane also attributed to her not feeling well: The will of a Leigh-Perrot uncle neglected to provide for the Austen family, particularly Mrs. Austen, his sister. Jane wrote to her brother Charles that the "shock" of this neglect caused her a "relapse" and she had sent for Cassandra to be with her, but now, she assured him, she was feeling better.

From the summer of 1816 through the rest of her life, most of the last of her surviving letters were to her nieces Fanny, Anna, and Caroline, and her nephew, James Edward. She wrote to them about family, about love, and about writing. She also downplayed her illness and focused on the care her family gave her. In a letter to her friend Anne Sharp telling her that she'd be going to Winchester to seek advice of doctors there, Austen joked, "I am now really a very genteel, portable sort of an Invalid." And in her last letter to James Edward, she wrote on a more serious note: "If ever you are ill, may you be as tenderly nursed as I have been . . . & may you possess—as I dare say you will—the greatest blessing of all, in the consciousness of not being unworthy of their Love.—I could not feel this." But mostly, she used her letters with friends and family to simply spend time with them.

LITERARY CONNECTIONS

A key literary innovation by Jane Austen is what scholars refer to as "free indirect discourse." Through this technique, the narrative takes readers from the objective viewpoint of the narrator to the subjective thoughts of a specific character. This technique is used to help readers get a deeper sense of a character, like Austen's heroine Anne Elliot, who thinks to herself of a grieving friend that "he has not, perhaps, a more sorrowing heart than I have."

A Final (Unfinished) Novel

In January 1817, Jane Austen sat down for the last time to begin a novel. She called it *The Brothers*, and wrote eleven and a half chapters before her illness forced her to abandon the project. What exists of *The Brothers* (later published as *Sanditon*) suggests it's about illness, greed, assumptions, and hope, all playing out in one place: Sanditon. Just like any Austen novel, it includes a young, astute heroine: Charlotte Heywood. Along her way to forging a path to stability, Charlotte encounters absurdities, gossip, and wild speculation.

Scholars have little to go on from this unfinished novel, and Austen struggled to write it while ill, but one passage is thought to provide a key. It involves a carriage ride on the way to Sanditon, with Charlotte Heywood riding alongside Tom Parker, whose "highest claims," including "those of his birthplace, property, and home," have all been replaced by his new life, based on speculation and business, in Sanditon. Parker's wife is also traveling in the carriage. Looking out the window, Charlotte notices a "very snug-looking place . . . well fenced and planted, and rich in the garden, orchard and meadows." This turns out to be Tom Parker's birthplace and family home, which he and his wife have left so he can pursue his financial prospects in Sanditon. As they drive by,

Mrs. Parker notes that it has "such an excellent garden," and she turns to look out the back window with "something like the fondness of regret."

In this simple description of a snug cottage and a young wife looking back *regretfully* through a carriage window, readers may well have the key to Austen's final novel: the contrast between the comfort and security of a familiar space and the risk, greed, and misplaced ambition that will come to embody everything in Sanditon. At a time when her own health was failing, Austen's story about looking back and past regrets is poignant.

THE MORE YOU KNOW

Jane Austen enthusiasts have noticed that Austen uses quite a few words about knowledge and misinformation in her novel fragment, *The Brothers* (later published as *Sanditon*). One passage alone includes the words *incongruity, ignorance, blunders, vigilance, caution, clear-sighted,* and *infallible*. The narrator of this novel consistently calls attention to the processes of reasoning, knowing, and belief.

A Call Back to Steventon

Jane Austen had her own experiences to draw from about the contentments of home and the instability of leaving all that behind when she was writing *Sanditon.* Back in November 1800, just before her parents had suddenly announced that the family would be leaving Steventon parsonage to move to Bath, a twenty-four-year-old Jane wrote Cassandra about their home and its comforts: "The Tables are come, and give general contentment," and she added, "the two ends put together form our constant table for everything."

Her letter continued into the next day, when she wrote that a severe storm had passed through Steventon: "I was sitting alone in the dining-room, when an odd kind of crash startled me . . . ; I then went to the window, which I reached just in time to see the last of our two highly valued Elms descend into the Sweep!!!!!!" The storm had damaged a spruce fir, two chestnuts, and a large elm on the property. Austen described these trees as things she had grown up with and valued—and now were gone.

Austen's final novel depicts the abandonment of a family home "rich in the garden, orchard and meadows." Although the novel would never be finished, it's possible her final heroine was going to choose family, preservation, and nature over the speculative ambitions of that new town called Sanditon. It's possible that she was thinking about her own childhood home as she wrote these first pages of *Sanditon.*

LITERARY CONNECTIONS

In *Sanditon,* when Charlotte Heywood is confronted with Mr. Arthur Parker and his theory that green tea gives him an ache in his side, she says she wishes people would simply consult "those who have studied right sides and green tea scientifically and thoroughly understand all the possibilities of their action on each other." It's one of many instances in the unfinished novel where Jane Austen addresses the theme of misinformation and using logic to tackle rumors.

Introducing Miss Georgiana Lambe

Outside the cottage where Jane Austen wrote *Mansfield Park*, *Emma*, and *Persuasion*, and was now writing the first pages of *Sanditon*, her own family was dealing with deepening financial crises, like Henry's bank declaring bankruptcy.

And while she was facing these crises, the characters of her current novel were also focused on money matters. In fact, Sanditon, the setting of *The Brothers*, was founded on speculation and finance. In order to pay back the money the founders had invested, they needed Sanditon to be a trendy destination. It needed to attract fashionable—and more importantly, rich—people . . . like the Miss Beauforts. These "Misses" are described as "very accomplished and very ignorant," and invite a comparison to a letter Jane had written back in Bath in 1808. In this letter to Cassandra, she had described a gathering where she found herself "tricked into a thorough party . . . The Miss [Maitlands] were as civil & as silly as usual."

But apart from the "ignorant" Misses, there's one character that Sanditon's residents are fascinated by: Miss Georgiana Lambe. The narrator says Lambe, a seventeen-year-old heiress, "had an immense fortune—richer than all the rest—and very delicate health." Before she arrives, rumors have been spreading all over town about who she is, how much she's worth, and more. When she finally comes to town, she is "beyond comparison the most important and precious . . . She was . . . to have the best room in the lodgings, and was also of the first consequence in every plan."

Some believe the character of Georgiana Lambe may have been inspired by the oppression Jane Austen had witnessed since childhood—and by abolitionists like Olaudah Equiano who were speaking out for freedom. By 1817, Jane Austen had read countless books about slavery (which wouldn't be abolished in the British Empire until years after her passing), and in her very last novel, she was creating a character that overturns expectations and provides a remarkable vision: of a young Black woman holding the power to save a misguided town—an enigmatic beauty who is the first consequence in every plan.

The More You Know

Olaudah Equiano was an abolitionist speaker and writer in eighteenth-century England who wrote the first globally famous narrative of slavery, *The Interesting Narrative of the Life of Olaudah Equiano, or Gustavus Vassa, the African*. The narrative provides a description of life in Nigeria and a firsthand account of the global slave trade. It was published in 1789, when Jane Austen was just thirteen years old.

From Sanditon

Mrs. Griffiths was a very well-behaved, genteel kind of woman, who supported herself by receiving such great girls and young ladies, as wanted either masters for finishing their education, or a home for beginning their displays - She had several more under her care than the three who were now come to Sanditon, but the others all happened to be absent. - Of these three, and indeed of all, Miss Lambe was beyond comparison the most important and precious, as she paid in proportion to her fortune. - She was about seventeen, half mulatto, chilly and tender, had a maid of her own, was to have the best room in the lodgings, and was also of the first consequence in every plan of Mrs. Griffiths.

The other girls, two Miss Beauforts, were just such young ladies as may be met with, in at least one family out of three, throughout the kingdom; they had tolerable complexions, showy figures, an upright decided carriage and an assured look; - they were very accomplished and very ignorant . . .

Writers in Training

In early 1817, Jane Austen was still writing letters with her usual levity and liveliness, including correspondence with her nephew, James Edward Austen-Leigh, now nineteen years old. He was now sending her his own fictional works! Even as she struggled with her health and with writing her novel *Sanditon*, she shared her methods and ideas on writing fiction with her nephew. "What should I do with your strong, manly, spirited Sketches, full of variety & Glow?" she wrote. "How could I possibly join them on to the little bit (two Inches wide) of Ivory on which I work with so fine a Brush, as produces little effect after much labour?" Her self-deprecating humor seems to have been intended to boost her nephew's confidence.

A niece, Caroline, was also sending samples of her writing to her aunt at this time. In one reply, Austen wrote, "I wish I could finish stories as fast as you can," praising Caroline's writing that is "so much alive upon any topic of such absurdity, as the usual description of a Heroine's father.—You have done it full justice." But it was to another niece, Anna, now married to Ben Lefroy, that Austen gave a deeper insight into her method of novel writing. Back when she was in the midst of writing *Emma* in the autumn of 1814, she advised Anna, "You are now collecting your People delightfully, getting them exactly into such a spot as is the delight of my life;—3 or 4 Families in a Country Village, is the very thing to work on." As important as Austen's copious correspondence with her sister is to the fans who want to know more about her, some of the clearest insights into how Austen felt about art, people, family, and love come from her surviving letters to her nieces Anna, Fanny, and Caroline, and nephew James Edward.

LITERARY CONNECTIONS

Punctuation can be just as important as word choice to the meaning of a writer's work, and for Jane Austen, it was a tool for conveying her signature wit. For instance, when Lord Byron was publishing sweeping verse tales like *The Corsair*, Austen wrote to Cassandra apologizing for multiple letters and explaining: "I have read the Corsair, mended my petticoat, & have nothing left to do." By linking them with a comma, she equates the work of this Romantic celebrity poet with household work like mending underwear!

Fanny Knight, an Austen Heroine

During Jane Austen's final year, Cassandra was staying by her side, so many of Jane's known letters from the time were to her niece Fanny Knight. These letters are filled with Jane's thoughts about romance, imagination, the life of a heroine, and Fanny herself: "You are inimitable, irresistible. You are the delight of my Life," she wrote to Fanny in February 1817, continuing: "Such Letters, such entertaining Letters as you have lately sent!"

At the time, Fanny had learned that her former suitor, Mr. Plumptre, was going to be married soon, and as she wrote in her diaries, she was regretting her decision to turn him down. Did she forgo her last chance for love?

But Jane Austen reassured her niece about her own choices and offered some advice about leaning on logic when she was unsure: "Spread no such malicious slander upon your Understanding, within the Precincts of your Imagination.—Do not speak ill of your Sense, merely for the Gratification of your Fancy." Her aunt was telling her to trust herself.

As Austen enthusiasts have pointed out, it's advice that drew from her own lifelong study of character, motivation, feeling, and reason when it came to love. Austen even connected Fanny to the characters she wrote about, telling her in a letter the following month, "You may perhaps like the Heroine [of *Persuasion*], as she is almost too good for me." At a time when her health was failing, Austen was passing on her wisdom, creativity, and love. "It is very, very gratifying to me to know you so intimately," Austen wrote in her February letter. "You can hardly think what a pleasure it is to me, to have such thorough pictures of your Heart."

The More You Know

In her very last letter to Fanny Knight, Jane Austen confided that she had a new novel ready (*Persuasion*) and that not many people knew about it. She had only told her brother Henry, because "I could not say No when he asked me, but he knows nothing more of it."

Illness

On March 18, Jane Austen stopped working on her latest novel, *Sanditon*, and that May, she went with Cassandra to receive medical treatment in Winchester. According to her letters that month, she was experiencing fevers, fatigue, "rheumatism," and "black and white" patches on her skin. In Winchester, she stayed at a "very Comfortable" lodging on College Street where she got medical care and regular visits from her brothers Henry and James. That spring, Jane wrote to her friend Anne Sharp about her family's support: "Every dear Brother so affectionate & so anxious!—and as for my Sister!—Words must fail me in any attempt to describe what a nurse she has been to me."

But by the beginning of July, her siblings knew her condition was dire. According to the Chawton House website, Jane was experiencing a "gradual deterioration with weak pulse, progressing to almost continuous sleep." Edward went to Chawton to be with Mrs. Austen, who seems to have been shielded from knowing the degree of her youngest daughter's suffering. (Mrs. Austen would later write that she "was not prepared for the Blow.") James Austen's wife, Mary Lloyd, went to Winchester to help Cassandra with the night shifts caring for Jane. Charles Austen, who had been dealing with not just his own illness but also the illness of his seven-year-old-daughter, Harriet Jane, had rushed to visit Jane in Winchester in mid-June. His surviving diary from the time includes daily notes about how Jane was doing. On Thursday, June 19, one month before her death, he wrote, "Saw her twice & in the evening for the last time in this world as I greatly fear, the Doctor having no hope of her final recovery."

The More You Know

It was common during this period for people to be cared for outside hospitals, especially those dealing with a chronic illness and/or in the final stages of their life. While the specifics of Jane Austen's treatment aren't known, medical practices at the time included bloodletting, herbal remedies, and opium-based pain relievers.

Jane Austen's Death

July 15 is St. Swithin's Day in England; St. Swithin was the ninth-century bishop of Winchester, and the weather on his feast day, according to folklore, predicts the weather for the next forty days. On this Tuesday morning in 1817, Jane Austen took a moment to notice the rain and the celebrations, jotting down some humorous lines of verse to celebrate the day, and noting its "races & revels & dissolute measures."

According to Cassandra, Jane suffered a "seizure" that Thursday evening, but by six o'clock was "talking quietly" to her; however, the seizure returned and after Cassandra watched her sister: "She felt herself to be dying about half an hour before she became tranquil and apparently unconscious. During that half hour was her struggle, pour Soul! She said she could not tell us what she suffered, tho' she complained of little fixed pain." Dr. Lyford was called to give Jane something for the pain.

That evening, "by seven oclock [sic] at the latest," Jane was "in a state of quiet insensibility," for six hours, Cassandra wrote to their niece Fanny Knight. Cassandra "sat close to [Jane] with a pillow in my lap to assist in supporting her head" and at some point during the night their sister-in-law Mary took over for Cassandra for two and a half hours until,

Cassandra wrote, "I took it again & in about one hour more she breathed her last." It was the early morning of Friday, July 18, 1817. An official cause of death remains undetermined, though there are theories that it was Addison's disease, Hodgkin's disease, or lupus.

In that same letter to Fanny, Cassandra wrote, "I have lost a treasure, such a Sister, such a friend as can never have been surpassed,—She was the sun of my life, the gilder of every pleasure, the soother of every sorrow . . . " She also acknowledged Fanny's feelings, reassuring her niece that she was "double dear to me now for her dear sake whom we have lost," adding, "She did love you most sincerely."

THE MORE YOU KNOW

Jane Austen is buried in the north aisle of the nave of Winchester Cathedral, where her gravestone pays tribute to "the extraordinary endowments of her mind," but makes no specific mention of her achievements as a novelist. It wasn't until decades later that a brass plaque would be placed near her gravesite commemorating Jane Austen as "Known to many by her writings."

Memories and Mementos

On July 29, 1817, from Chawton, Cassandra wrote to Fanny about Jane's funeral service, held by family on July 24. According to English custom at this time, she had taken some locks of Jane's hair to place into mementos. Jane's brothers, Edward, Henry, and Frank, conveyed the coffin to Winchester Cathedral, arriving so quietly, according to Cassandra, that she "should not have known when they left the House." The brothers carried the coffin down College Street toward the cathedral, until, Cassandra wrote, "it turned from my sight & I had lost her forever . . ."

Cassandra and family friend Martha Lloyd continued living with Mrs. Austen at Chawton Cottage until Mrs. Austen's death in 1827, at the age of 87. The next year, Martha moved out when she married Frank Austen. Cassandra continued to live at Chawton Cottage until her own death in 1845, at the age of 72. According to Jane Austen's House museum, Cassandra kept bees and a garden and taught local children in her remaining years. She also enjoyed the companionship of a dog named Link, who would help a manservant get milk from a nearby farm, carrying the milk pail home in his mouth.

Brother James Austen had passed on in 1819. The rest of the Austen siblings would continue passing over the next several decades: George in 1838, Henry in 1850, Edward and Charles in 1852, and Frank in 1865. Before her own death, Cassandra would put together a collection of family mementos for Jane's nieces and nephews. Charles's daughters Cassy and Fanny received locks of Jane's hair set in pearls and Cassandra's topaz cross respectively. The contents of a small bureau drawer—including the early draft of *Persuasion*'s final chapter—went to Anna. Cassandra burned "the greatest part" of Jane's letters and also snipped out or censored parts of other letters—presumably to protect the reputation of Jane and other family members. She divided the surviving letters between Caroline, Cassy, Frank's daughters, and Fanny. James Edward would eventually ask Anna, Caroline, and Fanny for their memories and letters for a biography he was writing about his aunt.

THE MORE YOU KNOW

Jane Austen's nephew James Edward Austen-Leigh became a member of the clergy in 1822 against the wishes of wealthy Austen aunt Mrs. Leigh-Perrot, who apparently threatened to "do nothing for him in the future" if he pursued the clergy. James Edward went ahead with his choice, married a woman named Emma Smith in 1828, and inherited the Leigh-Perrot estate of Scarlets in 1838 (with the provision that he take on the name "Leigh" with Austen).

From Northanger Abbey, Chapter 5

"It is only a novel!" . . . or, in short, only some work in which the greatest powers of the mind are displayed, in which the most thorough knowledge of human nature, the happiest delineation of its varieties, the liveliest effusions of wit and humour, are conveyed to the world in the best-chosen language.

A "Spinster" Legacy

Before the year 1817 reached its close, Henry Austen worked to have a four-volume edition of his sister's works published, on commission, with John Murray. The edition contained *Northanger Abbey* in the first two volumes, followed by *Persuasion* in the second two volumes. He included a "biographical notice" identifying Jane as the author of her previously anonymous novels and emphasizing the respectability, sweetness, and long-suffering Christian spirit of his sister.

In the spring of 1818, the two final contemporary reviews of Austen's works had emerged, and each took a different perspective. One negative review in the *British Critic* would stick to Austen's legacy for more than a century: "In imagination, of all kinds, she appears to have been extremely deficient; not only her stories are utterly and entirely devoid of invention, but her characters, her incidents, her sentiments, are obviously all drawn exclusively from experience . . . "

A second reviewer in *Edinburgh Magazine* praised Austen and her novels: "We have always regarded her works as possessing a higher claim to public estimation than perhaps they have yet attained." The reviewer compared Austen's works, now considered innovators of the novel of social realism, to the works of Sir Walter Scott and Lord Byron and their "high-wrought passions," and looked toward "the time . . . when we shall take a more permanent delight in those familiar cabinet pictures, than even in the great historical pieces of our more eminent modern masters. . . . When this period arrives, we have no hesitation in saying, that the delightful writer of the works now before us, will be one of the most popular of English novelists . . . " Austen herself had invited this comparison in *Persuasion*, with allusions to a dynamic not only in art but in personal philosophy between the "high-wrought passions" and quiet reason and reflection.

Literary Connections

Novelist Henry James, who noted Austen as inspiration for his own novels of class, society, and love—and even while viewing her as setting the standard for novels—referred to her as "dear old Jane" and insisted that her art arose not from imaginative genius, but rather from a sort of unconscious soaking up of her environment, saying that she "fell a-musing" "over her work-basket."

Reading and Writing Aunt Jane

As the public interest in Austen's novels continued to grow into the latter half of the nineteenth century and the Victorian era, Austen's family shared memories and even continued reading her stories aloud together. Cassandra Austen made frequent, lengthy visits to Frank Austen and Lady Austen/Martha Lloyd at their estate Portsdown Lodge, where Austen scholar Deirdre Le Faye writes that they enjoyed family readings of the novels with Frank's daughters Cassy Eliza, Catherine Anne, and Fanny Sophia. Cassandra's close relationships with her nieces and nephews allowed for more information about Jane Austen's life to gradually emerge over the years following her death. (Caroline Austen wrote of a candid, sudden announcement one day from her aunt Cassandra that Jane had conducted a "seaside romance" in the early 1800s at one of the Austen family's seaside holidays!)

Eventually, the trio of James Austen's children, James Edward, Caroline, and Anna—at James Edward's instigation—put these shared memories to work in publication. First came James Edward's *A Memoir of Jane Austen*. Published on December 16, 1869, James, Caroline, and Anna all contributed to the memories and letters compiled in this book. Charles's daughter Cassy Esten also contributed. Caroline compiled a second memoir, called *My Aunt Jane Austen,* that would be published posthumously on January 1, 1952. Caroline herself would never marry, living with her mother in the country until her death in 1880.

Subsequent generations, including Fanny Knight's son Lord Brabourne, continued to share memories and artifacts of Jane's legacy. Lord Brabourne published the letters that Cassandra had entrusted to his mother, Fanny Knight, in 1884. James Edward's daughter, Mary Augusta Austen-Leigh, published another memoir, *Personal Aspects of Jane Austen,* in 1920. Le Faye, an administrator at the British Museum, worked with descendants of Richard Arthur Austen-Leigh to compile and organize selections of family correspondence and diaries into the 1989 book *Jane Austen: A Family Record.* And in 2018, Edward Knight's direct descendent, Caroline Knight, released the memoir *Jane & Me: My Austen Heritage.*

THE MORE YOU KNOW

The family lore about Jane's mysterious seaside romance has inhabited an afterlife in Austen screen biopics, such as the 2025 BBC/PBS series *Miss Austen.*

A Lasting Impact on Romantic Fiction

The genre of fiction known today as the rom-com has a standard formula. According to Pamela Regis in her *A Natural History of the Romance Novel,* it follows six steps or "beats": (1) The setting is established. (2) Two people who obviously should be together for whatever reason meet and are attracted to each other. (3) An obstacle to their romance is presented. (4) A disruption in the culture, society, or family of the characters occurs. (5) A literal or figurative brush with death makes all appear hopeless for the lovers. (6) Finally, reconciliation restores stability to the lovers, their family, and their community.

Not only can these beats of the rom-com be seen in Jane Austen's novels, but she is credited with innovating this formula! After establishing the setting—a community and its values—the meetup between two characters who are clearly meant to be together usually takes place in her novels, whether it's a smoldering encounter across an assembly room ball like with Mr. Darcy and Elizabeth Bennet, or when someone practically lives in your house like Emma's Mr. Knightley. Next in the rom-com structure are the obstacles to love that are presented, like the lovers' own personalities, pride and prejudices, or the hostility of family (as in the case of Henry Tilney and Catherine Morland, as well as Edward Ferrars and Elinor Dashwood).

The rom-com landmark that Regis describes as a "disordering" of the setting comes next: This is the Dashwood family hysterics after Edward Ferrars's secret fiancée, Lucy Steele, is found out, or Emma's rudeness at the Box Hill picnic. The disruption turns social order upside down in a way that subverts expectations and makes the outcome of the story less predictable. After this event comes what Regis calls the "ritual death," where all appears to be lost: Lydia has run away with Mr. Wickham and disgraced the Bennet family forever, while Frederick Wentworth will marry Louisa after her near-fatal fall from the Cobb. But things suddenly turn around. Misunderstandings, disgrace, and banishments are resolved, and the two lovers come together for what Regis calls "reconciliation," that brings the most important rom-com component of all: a happily-ever-after.

The More You Know

Most of Austen's novels have been adapted into musicals: *Pride and Prejudice, Sense and Sensibility, Emma, Persuasion,* and *Mansfield Park* (also adapted as an opera).

An Iconic White Shirt and an Austen Adaptation

Jane Austen's novels have been celebrated through screen adaptations, retellings, and fan fictions since the twentieth century, and her stories continue to inspire to this day! The most famous adaptation of her work was the BBC series *Pride and Prejudice*. Released in 1995, this six-episode series features Jennifer Ehle as lively and intelligent Elizabeth Bennet, and Colin Firth as a commanding but vulnerable Mr. Darcy. It set the standard for screen adaptations of Jane Austen's work, and it was a sensation in the UK almost before it hit the screen. Leading up to the premiere on the BBC, screenwriter Andrew Davies gave interviews that led to sensational headlines about the sexiness of Austen. Davies was describing his approach more than anything that would be on screen, but the stage was set: By the time the first episode hit, audiences were primed and expecting to see smoldering desire.

And the series didn't disappoint. Episode four featured what some consider the most iconic scene in all of the Austen on-screen canon: the wet shirt scene. In this scene, Mr. Darcy, thinking that he's alone on his estate at Pemberley, takes a dive into a private lake to cool off after going for a horseback ride. Austen history was made when Colin Firth emerged from the water in a dripping-wet long white shirt and walked across the Pemberley grounds—to encounter an astonished Elizabeth. Screenwriter Andrew Davies later said the scene was part of a bid to provide an inner life for the elusive hero. The lake encounter is awkward for both characters in the adaptation, and while it isn't included in Austen's novel, it brings out a shared vulnerability in Darcy and Elizabeth.

The More You Know

In April 2025, members of the cast and crew got together for a conversation about the 1995 *Pride and Prejudice* series during its thirtieth anniversary. In this BBC program called *The Reunion*, screenwriter Andrew Davies said he had initially insisted that Colin Firth should be naked for the iconic lake scene, but producer Sue Birtwistle insisted that having the actor in wet clothes would actually be sexier.

Mr. Darcy's Hand Flex

A second popular adaptation of *Pride and Prejudice* came in 2005. Directed by Joe Wright, this film stars Keira Knightley as Elizabeth Bennet and Matthew Macfadyen as Mr. Darcy. Filmed primarily in the English counties of Northamptonshire, Lincolnshire, Derbyshire, Wiltshire, Berkshire, and Kent, this adaptation was generally well received, particularly by younger, mainstream audiences. Some viewers feel it is more accessible than the 1995 adaptation, despite being seen as less accurate to the book's plot.

But it was a single gesture by actor Matthew Macfadyen that has become iconic for Austen fans: a hand flex. In fact, this gesture has come to symbolize the restraint and the tension of Austenian passions. The flex was actually improvised, Macfadyen later told NPR, in a rehearsal where the director, noticing it, requested the team to "Get that!" In the final cut, Macfadyen's hand flex appears during a scene that comes just after Elizabeth's humiliating visit to the Bingley estate of Netherfield. Elizabeth visits Netherfield when Jane is stranded there sick, and the sisters face the "superciliousness" and snobbery of Caroline Bingley. But while Elizabeth feels humiliated during this visit, she holds her own, and Darcy notices. When they all take their leave, tensions smolder, and after touching Elizabeth's hand to help her into the carriage, Macfadyen's hand flexes as he walks back to the house. It's a scene beloved by many Austen fans that captures all the frustration, anguish, brooding, and passion in Darcy in one tense and now notorious gesture.

The More You Know

Matthew Macfadyen told *Fresh Air*'s Dave Davies that when it came to playing Mr. Darcy, his "confidence wasn't great." He explained, "I didn't feel I was dishy enough and sort of brooding enough." But Macfadyen said he leaned into the "tortured adolescent" vibe of Mr. Darcy, and fans loved it.

An Award-Winning Sense and Sensibility Adaptation

When the subject of Austen film adaptations comes up, many times it's the scenes involving Colin Firth in a wet white tunic or Matthew Macfadyen walking toward Keira Knightley across a field at dawn that get the spotlight. But the most applauded film adaptation of an Austen novel might actually be the 1995 production of *Sense and Sensibility*, directed by Ang Lee, with a screenplay by Emma Thompson (who also starred as Elinor).

Lee, a Taiwan-born filmmaker who studied film at the University of Illinois and New York University, had spent years directing films about intergenerational Chinese families before taking on this adaptation of Austen's classic. For *Sense and Sensibility*, Lee brought his eye for family drama and rich cultural backdrops to an English period piece. He was nominated for many awards for his work on the film, including the BAFTA, Golden Globe, and Directors Guild Award for best director. He won the Golden Bear (the highest prize for best film) at the Berlin International Film Festival that year.

Emma Thompson was also nominated for several awards for both her acting and screenwriting, and won an Oscar for Best Adapted Screenplay and a Golden Globe for Best Screenplay—just to name a couple! She had spent five years writing and revising the screenplay, which was her first ever. In fact, studios were hesitant to take on the film with Thompson as the credited writer since she didn't have any previous writing credits. Luckily, Columbia Pictures eventually agreed to distribute *Sense and Sensibility.*

The film also included other well-known British actors like Imelda Staunton (Charlotte Palmer), Harriet Walter (Fanny Dashwood), Alan Rickman (Colonel Brandon), Kate Winslet (Marianne), Hugh Grant (Edward Ferrars), and Hugh Laurie (Mr. Palmer). Recognized as one of the best Austen adaptations of all time, the star-studded cast and screenplay helped inspire new popularity for Austen's novels.

THE MORE YOU KNOW

Love was brewing on the set of *Sense and Sensibility*! The project inspired a real-life romance between Emma Thompson and Greg Wise, who played the brooding John Willoughby. The two married in 2003.

Austenland

"I'm going to take charge of my story!" So announces Jane, the protagonist of the 2013 film *Austenland,* directed by Jerusha Hess and coproduced by Stephenie Meyer of Twilight fame. Adapted from Shannon Hale's 2007 novel of the same name, this twist on Austen's classics follows Jane, a modern young woman obsessed with *Pride and Prejudice.* In the story, she embarks on a holiday at a Jane Austen theme park in search of herself—and love. The vacation involves specially customized experiences on an English country estate—from rural walks to proper teas—curated for customers like Jane and her fellow traveler Miss Elizabeth Charming, played by Jennifer Coolidge. Like an Austen heroine, *Austenland*'s Jane, played by Keri Russell, encounters a lineup of Austen situations, stock characters, and potential heroes on this holiday—like Henry Nobley (played by JJ Feild, who also played Henry Tilney in the 2007 *Northanger Abbey* movie adaptation).

Austenland is part of a growing collection that explore not so much Austen's work, but aspects of the Jane Austen fandom itself. The 2025 film *Jane Austen Wrecked My Life,* by French director Laura Piani, also explores the impact of Austen's work on a young person's life and love. In this movie,

Agathe, played by Camille Rutherford, is a Parisian bookseller and Austen devotee, who takes up a writer's residency at an English estate run and owned by family descendants of Jane Austen—including Oliver, a dreamboat Austen great-nephew played by Charlie Anson.

Both *Austenland*'s Jane and *Jane Austen Wrecked My Life*'s Agathe get their happily-ever-after in films that each explore the conflict between romanticism and pragmatism. These movies tap into that blend of ironic distance and soulful yearning that is right off the pages of Jane Austen's work.

LITERARY CONNECTIONS

There are also several books that explore the Jane Austen fandom. These include *Among the Janeites* by Deborah Yaffe and *The Jane Austen Society* by Natalie Jenner.

An LGBTQIA+ Retelling

One of the best tributes to the universality of the themes of Austen's novels is the way retellings of these stories have been adapted to various communities and countless settings, from Soniah Kamal's *Unmarriageable,* set in Pakistan; and Ibi Zoboi's *Pride,* set in Brooklyn, New York; to Sonali Dev's *Incense and Sensibility, The Emma Project,* and *Recipe for Persuasion.*

In Joel Kim Booster's *Fire Island,* directed by Andrew Ahn, the themes of snobbery, money, and opposites attracting in *Pride and Prejudice* are transferred to LGBTQIA+ party haven Fire Island. Here a group of longtime friends socialize, strategize, and bid for love. Writer and creator Booster said he once took a copy of Jane Austen's *Pride and Prejudice* with him on a trip to Fire Island; overlapping the characters of Elizabeth and Darcy with characters in *Fire Island* came organically.

In *Fire Island,* the Elizabeth Bennet character is Noah, a clever, earnest nurse insulted by but unable to look away from pediatrician Will (representing Mr. Darcy), with his entourage of haughty friends. The two clash, tensions smolder, and their feelings come out in a scene that pays homage to Joe Wright's 2005 *Pride & Prejudice,* when Will and Noah confront each other as well as their own anxieties about social status, rejection, and more contemporary problems like modern drugs during a shouting match in the rain. Just as with Matthew Macfadyen and Keira Knightley in the 2005 film, the scene shifts between hostility and romantic tension. Of course, Noah and Will get their happily-ever-after—and one with all the harmony of an Austen ending, featuring a romantic sunset shared with friends.

THE MORE YOU KNOW

Directors Joe Wright and Andrew Ahn may or may not have realized how impactful storms were in Jane Austen's world. Throughout her letters and novels, weather has an impact on human activity and feelings. In May 1811, she described her "uncomfortable feelings" in a thunderstorm, and how her anxiety was assuaged by "Blinds & Candles." The impact of rainstorms would come up again and again in her novels.

Love, Romance, and Horror

Jane Austen's way of working through the dangers, oppressions, and power structures of her day is through parody and comedy. But these forces also can be dealt with handily through horror. Titles like *Bespelling Jane Austen, Pulse and Prejudice, Mr. Darcy, Vampyre,* and an entire series of retellings from Quirk Books that includes *Pride and Prejudice and Zombies* and *Sense and Sensibility and Sea Monsters* (both released in 2009), layer the formulas of the horror genre on to Austen's six novels.

In Seth Grahame-Smith's *Pride and Prejudice and Zombies,* Elizabeth and her sisters are still trying to navigate the social and romantic realms of nineteenth-century England—this time during a zombie apocalypse! Elizabeth and Darcy, and Jane and Bingley, still get their happily-ever-after, despite the continuing zombie attacks. Meanwhile, in *Sense and Sensibility and Sea Monsters,* an event known as "The Alteration" has turned sea creatures against humans. Elinor and Marianne battle octopuses, giant lobsters, and pirates, eventually uniting with their true loves, Edward Ferrars and the part-human part-squid Colonel Brandon. Both retellings have been generally well received, and *Pride and Prejudice and Zombies* was even adapted into a movie in 2016. *Bespelling Jane Austen*; *Pulse and Prejudice*; *Mr. Darcy*; and *Vampyre* all follow Mr. Darcy as a vampire who tries to overcome his bloodlust and find a cure.

The combination of romance and horror in titles like *Pride and Prejudice and Zombies* seems to resonate with fans because some of the best works of genre fiction—in literature and film, and in comedy and horror—unveil hidden powers, desires, and dangers in life. These fictions help readers confront their fears and have some fun in a way that vanquishes evil. And whether it's *Northanger Abbey*'s Catherine Morland wandering forbidden corridors or Elizabeth Bennet confronting snobbery, Austen's own characters confront their demons.

THE MORE YOU KNOW

In 1815 and 1816 while Jane Austen was at a height of writing, publishing, proofing pages, and chasing publishers, a young Mary Shelley was weaving a tale of her own: the horror story *Frankenstein*. Today, Shelley's monster is just as beloved as Austen's heroines.

The Road to Bridgerton

Bridgerton arrived on Netflix in December 2020 and quickly became the streaming service's biggest hit at the time. And even though the show has plenty of on-screen sex—along with twists that turn the Regency world upside down—there's also a lot of Jane Austen to be found in *Bridgerton*. Based on the romance novels by Julia Quinn and created by Shonda Rhimes (of *Grey's Anatomy*, *Scandal*, and much more), the series mainly evokes the world of Jane Austen through its setting: the Regency era. The characters in *Bridgerton* take part in court visits and courtships, elaborate eighteenth-century rituals, and the restrictive social conventions of this time period.

Bridgerton captures the era Austen herself spent a lifetime experiencing and writing about: a time of heady romantic ideals, gossip, chaperones, balls, grand estates, drawing room decorum, and more. Reflecting Austen's works, this popular series follows the Bridgerton siblings and their suitors as they find love among all the social etiquette and expectations. There's the swagger and entitlement of an eldest son in Anthony Bridgerton, a spirited heroine pushing boundaries in the character of Daphne Bridgerton, and plenty of Regency activities, from reciting poetry to flirting at balls.

There are also Austen-inspired plot points like family disapprovals, status and court, and miscommunications.

But not only does the *Bridgerton* series re-create Austen's world: It also reimagines it. *Bridgerton* includes a cast of racially diverse characters and an alternative take on racial history. In this story, King George III has married a woman of African descent, Queen Charlotte, and granted aristocratic titles (such as Lord, Duke, and Viscount) to many people with African heritage. Through its unique twists on the time, *Bridgerton* challenges the real world as Jane herself did through her novels.

THE MORE YOU KNOW

The word *colonialism*—denoting a policy of expanding the British Empire that formed a backdrop to Austen's novels—is not used by Jane Austen, but post-colonial studies of her works have largely followed in the wake of the writings of Edward Said and his approach to Austen. One of the earliest references of the word, according to the *Oxford English Dictionary*, is from British philosopher and reformer Jeremy Bentham in a letter from 1791, when Austen was fifteen years old.

From Persuasion, Chapter 24

Who can be in doubt of what followed? When any two young people take it into their heads to marry, they are pretty sure by perseverance to carry their point, be they ever so poor, or ever so imprudent, or ever so little likely to be necessary to each other's ultimate comfort. This may be bad morality to conclude with, but I believe it to be truth; and if such parties succeed, how should a Captain Wentworth and an Anne Elliot, with the advantage of maturity of mind, consciousness of right, and one independent fortune between them, fail of bearing down every opposition?

Austen Societies and Celebrations

Along with the many adaptations of Austen's novels over the years have come a number of societies in her honor. One main example is the Jane Austen Society. Founded in the UK in 1940, this society preserves Austen-related sites such as Chawton Cottage and shares her works with the public. In addition to annual meetings and lectures, the Jane Austen Society publishes the "Jane Austen Society Report" each year, featuring dozens of illustrated articles about Austen's life and writing.

Another popular society is the Jane Austen Society of North America (JASNA), founded in 1979. Each year, JASNA and its some five thousand members host a huge gathering known as the Annual General Meeting—or AGM. This meeting includes not only a roster of international Austen scholars from across the globe, but also a grand ball hosted on one of its final evenings. Academics, independent scholars, Janeites, podcasters, readers, cosplayers, and fans gather for scholarly presentations and dialogue by day and Regency-style dancing by night. Workshops on bonnet making, corset making, turban tying, and English country dancing are enthusiastically attended by global scholars and readers alike. There are also popular Jane Austen societies in Australia (the Jane Austen Society of Australia) and Japan (the Jane Austen Society of Japan).

And although there is no official holiday for Jane Austen, there are several annual festivals held in her honor. The Jane Austen Festival takes place in Bath, England, each September. Featuring Regency costumes, dancing, and discussions, it lasts for about ten days and is the largest Austen celebration in the world. Meanwhile, the Jane Austen Festival Australia takes place in Canberra, Australia, each April, and includes Regency-era fashion shows, high tea, balls, and lectures. Fans around the world also celebrate Jane Austen's birthday with book readings, tea parties, and social media tributes.

The More You Know

The Bank of England issued a new official £10 note in 2017. First released two hundred years after her death, this note features a portrait of Jane Austen.

Further Reading and Listening

BOOKS

- *Jane Austen: A Life.* By Claire Tomalin. Vintage Books—This is a favorite biography among Austen scholars and fans. Author and journalist Claire Tomalin provides a thorough account of Austen's life.
- *Jane Austen: A Family Record.* By Deirdre Le Faye. Cambridge University Press—Austen scholars and researchers are indebted to Le Faye's research compiled into this volume, which is a key source for much of the information in this book.
- *Jane Austen and the Province of Womanhood.* By Alison G. Sulloway. University of Pennsylvania Press—Scholar Alison Sulloway thoughtfully assesses Austen and her works with a view toward feminist history and ideas.
- *Jane Austen's Letters.* 4th ed. Edited by Deirdre Le Faye. Oxford University Press—Dierdre Le Faye's collection of Austen's 161 letters, as well as her own meticulously researched notes, is essential for Austen fans.

- *Jane Austen's Wardrobe.* By Hilary Davidson. Yale University Press—Drawing on Austen's letters, this book by fashion historian and curator Hilary Davidson provides research highlighting the context for the things Austen wore.
- *Jane Austen: Women, Politics, and the Novel.* By Claudia L. Johnson. University of Chicago Press—Johnson's writings on Austen have made a powerful contribution to Austen scholarship, influencing Austen's place in feminist history and theory.
- *Pride and Protest.* By Nikki Payne. Berkley—Nikki Payne (a trained anthropologist with a Substack titled *Love Is Payne*) retells Jane Austen's stories in contemporary, diverse settings.

PODCASTS

- *Austen Chat* hosts lively, erudite conversations with Austen scholars across the globe. Produced by the Jane Austen Society of North America (JASNA), it's hosted by JASNA member Breckyn Wood.
- *The Austen Connection,* produced by Janet Lewis Saidi, explores all things Jane Austen. Some information in this book can be found on *The Austen Connection.*
- *Reclaiming Jane,* a "Jane Austen podcast for fans on the margins," is produced by Lauren Wethers and Emily Davis-Hale, and features in-depth, fun conversations about each of Austen's novels and her juvenilia.

- *The Thing about Austen*, produced by Zan Cammack and Diane Neu, examines themes from Austen and her era through the lens of material culture.

Websites and Blogs

- *Jane Austen & Co.* (https://janeaustenandco.org), run by Dr. Inger Brodey and a team of Austen scholars, hosts a global series of discussions on Austen studies, including its influential video series Race and the Regency (2021) and Asia and the Regency (2021–2022). It also hosts a Jane Austen Summer Program featuring lectures, workshops, discussions, and a Regency ball.
- *Jane Austen's House* (https://janeaustens.house/jane-austen/) is a virtual collection of Austen artifacts found at the Jane Austen's House museum, including letters, jewelry, and books—and the research providing context for them. The museum itself is located at the house where Austen lived and wrote, revised, and published many of her novels.
- *Reading with Austen* (https://readingwithausten.com) is a virtual re-creation of the shelves of Godmersham Library at Edward Austen Knight's Godmersham estate, where Austen spent many days writing and thinking. The "Principal Investigator" of the project is Peter Sabor.

Index

N

P